Birding the Delaware Valley Region

A Comprehensive Guide to Birdwatching in Southeastern Pennsylvania, Central and Southern New Jersey, and Northcentral Delaware

John J. Harding and
Justin J. Harding

Temple University Press

Philadelphia

Temple University Press, Philadelphia 19122
© 1980 by Temple University. All rights reserved
Published 1980
Printed in the United States of America

Maps by Michele Martin, from originals by John J. Harding

Drawings by Jane E. Nelson, from originals by Justin J. Harding (except
for the Least Bittern and Brant)

Library of Congress Cataloging in Publication Data

Harding, John J
  Birding the Delaware Valley region.

  Bibliography: p.
  Includes index.
  1. Bird Watching—Delaware Valley. I. Harding, Justin J., joint author.
II. Title.
QL683.D53H37   598'.07'234739   80-10279
ISBN 0-87722-179-0
ISBN 0-87722-182-0 pbk.

To Eleanor, whose constant support and behind-the-scenes
  assistance made this guide possible

To our parents, who kindled and nurtured our
  interest in birdwatching and set the
  stage for writing this guide

Contents

Maps

Birding the Delaware Valley Region

Map 1
The Delaware Valley Region

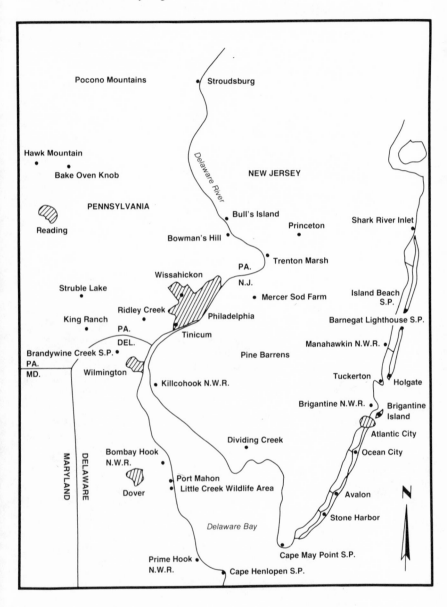

Introduction

Birdwatching is one of the fastest-growing hobbies in America. Recent estimates place the number of birdwatchers at between ten and twenty million people, depending on the criteria. Over 170 million dollars are spent annually on such birding-related paraphernalia and activities as binoculars, books, and tours. Reflecting the increased subscriptions to wildlife magazines and society memberships nationwide, many bird books are now in print. But while bird-finding guides have become increasingly popular, they usually concentrate on such "exotic" locations as Arizona, California, and Texas, places where unusual or accidental species can be found. This leaves many good areas without adequate coverage, for the few texts that deal with them tend to be either too limited in scope or too scholarly for the average birdwatcher. Little attention is paid to the practical details on how and where to find representative species.

The Delaware Valley region consists of southeastern Pennsylvania, central and southern New Jersey, and northcentral Delaware. With Philadelphia at its hub, the area has a long history steeped in birding tradition. The Academy of Natural Sciences was founded in 1812. The Delaware Valley Ornithological Club (D.V.O.C.), formed in 1890, is one of the oldest and most active birding organizations in the country. Today, the tri-state region has more than kept pace with the meteoric rise of birdwatching elsewhere. Many organizations and local chapters, along with an impressive lineup of both professional and amateur birders, monitor the area's rich avifauna.

Approximately four hundred species have been recorded in the Delaware Valley region. Diligent birdwatchers with many years in the field should approach 350 species on their regional life lists. Christmas Counts of 140 species are possible—especially near the Atlantic coast. Big Days in May tally between 120 and 170 species, depending on the location.

Within a hundred-mile radius of Philadelphia, a wealth of habitats and ecosystems are found. Mountains, deciduous woodlands, rolling meadows and farmlands, fresh-water lakes and marshes, river valleys, pine barrens, coastal beaches and wetlands, brackish estuaries, and the Atlantic Ocean attract a large and diverse bird population.

The Delaware Valley is blessed with many birding hot spots. National wildlife refuges, state parks, and other preserves are strategically located throughout the three states. All the region's varied habitats can be found in one or more of these sanctuaries. Many refuges have unique combinations of several diverse habitats within their boundaries. Most birds recorded in the tri-state area have been observed at one time or another in these special places. The advantages to the birds are protection, ideal location, and plentiful food and cover, all hard to come by these days. The advantage to the birder is the large number of species concentrated in a relatively small area.

Hopefully, these sanctuaries will remain free of outside encroachment, although increasing pollution always poses a threat. In a protected environment wildlife populations can stabilize, thus affording the birdwatcher a chance to make reliable and predictable observations over the years. Of course bird populations are dynamic, as are the various ecosystems. In a protected environment changes are gradual, so that periodic updates can reflect actual successions and transitions—barring natural disasters and man-made catastrophes.

Many scientific publications covering the region's birdlife are available. These works tend to emphasize the distinctive characteristics and habitats of individual species. Other texts, mainly periodicals and journals, highlight only the more interesting birds. But a systematic, comprehensive guide for finding the area's representative species is lacking. This book attempts to fill that need.

A comprehensive bird-finding guide should accent those places where most of the region's birds can reliably be found. Six major refuges are discussed in detail in this book. Other birding locations, which are closely related geographically or by tradition to the six major refuges, are also included. Religiously birding these areas over a five-year period should produce 90 percent or more of the Delaware Valley's representative species. Of the six, Hawk Mountain and Cape May Point State Park are internationally recognized. The remainder—Ridley Creek State Park, Tinicum Preserve, Brigantine National Wildlife Refuge, and Bombay Hook National Wildlife Refuge—are well known to local birdwatchers. All are within a two-hour drive of Philadelphia. This arbitrary two-hour cutoff allows most birders to plan day trips from Philadelphia without worrying about overnight accommodations. For visitors, Philadelphia has a large selection of motels, hotels, and restaurants to choose from. Various tour guides (such as A.A.A.) provide helpful information for planning extended stays. Another reason for extensive coverage of a few key areas is the gasoline shortage, and the possibility of strict gas rationing. Because most of the Delaware Valley's birds are seen at the six major refuges, it makes sense to concentrate on those places, rather than hop-skip around and waste precious fuel.

Another section of this guide covers an additional nineteen hot spots in less detail. These locations round out the region's birdwatching opportunities. Some are famous for great numbers of migrants funneling through small, discrete areas. Others cater to rare, unusual, or highly specialized birds not found elsewhere in the region. After these mini-chapters, passing reference is made to another 33 hot spots for the sake of completeness.

The annotated list of species toward the end of this guide enables the birdwatcher to crosscheck a particular species with the main text. In some instances, this list will be the only reference to where certain birds can be found. A short bibliography has been added to familiarize the birder with the pertinent literature in the field. Finally, an index makes possible quick and easy cross-referencing.

The information in this guide has been compiled over the past fifteen years. Our records of birds seen on regular field trips are the main source. This includes over 100 visits to several refuges, including Ridley Creek and Brigantine. Regional lists, plus the various refuge lists (if available), have been consulted. Years of informal communications with local birdwatchers add to the breadth and reliability of the data. Recently the Delaware Valley Birding Hot Line, a telephone rare bird alert, was set up to cover the tri-state area. This weekly service, sponsored jointly by the

D.V.O.C. and the Academy of Natural Sciences, highlights the previous week's more interesting sightings; call (215) 567-BIRD. The birding journals and texts covering the region have also been exhaustively read, and we have reviewed the Hudson-Delaware sections and local Christmas Counts in *American Birds* of the past eight years to crossvalidate our information.

Birdwatching in the Delaware Valley area is relatively uncomplicated. All the locations mentioned in this guide are easily accessible by car. Directions, maps, and topographical outlines of the various refuges are included in this book. At this time, all the refuges are free except for a nominal charge at Hawk Mountain Sanctuary. Binoculars (7×35, 8×40, 10×50) and a zoom scope are good investments. Popular bird identification guides include Peterson's *A Field Guide to the Birds* and Robbins's *Birds of North America*.

The weather is generally cooperative. Daytime temperatures in the summer are $75°-90°$ F, while the winter norms range between $25°$ and $45°$ F. Most refuges have excellent networks of foot trails and dikes, so walking shoes are usually adequate. Biting flies and mosquitoes are afield June through September, although this varies with the weather and the location. Repellent is a good idea —especially near the more coastal areas.

While birding is superb year-round, the greatest concentrations and number of species are seen during the spring and fall migrations. For waterfowl, this occurs March through mid-April and again October through November. Birds of prey abound in the autumn—September through November, depending on the species. Most shorebirds come through the area during the first three weeks in May. Their fall migration is more drawn out, starting in late July and ending in early October. The peak movement of spring landbirds also occurs during the first three weeks in May. Their autumn migration extends over a longer period too—usually from late August to early October. This is a general account, and detailed descriptions of terrain, faunal zones, and seasonal variations, along with more exact migration timetables, can be found in *Pennsylvania Birds*, by E. Poole, *Birds of Pennsylvania*, by M. Wood, *Bird Studies at Old Cape May*, by W. Stone, and *A Field List of Birds of the Delaware Valley Region*, by A. Brady et al.

Finally, this guide is designed to aid the "average" birdwatcher, although some of the material will appeal to both professional and beginner alike. Both the local birder familiar with the general area and the visiting birder can use this guide for more extensive coverage of the region's birds. Although successfully finding the area's representative species is less dramatic than finding rare or unusual birds, it is one of the most satisfying aspects of our addiction.

Ridley Creek State Park and Tyler Arboretum, Pennsylvania

Ridley Creek State Park

Ridley Creek State Park, only twenty miles west of center city Philadelphia, is a recently acquired 2,600-acre tract of deciduous woodlands and brushy meadows in Delaware County, Pennsylvania. In addition to several historical colonial buildings on the grounds, the park provides facilities for hiking, horseback riding, biking, and picnicking. Ridley Creek, a clear trout stream, bisects the park and attracts great numbers of both migrating and nesting landbirds. In particular, a short stretch of creek along Sycamore Mills Road in the extreme southeastern portion of the park is ideal for observing the area's representative birds. The remainder of Ridley Creek State Park, by far the largest part, is heavily used by picnickers and tourists and is reached through the main entrance off Route 3 (West Chester Pike). Birding has been done in this latter section, but it is now very crowded—especially on the weekends.

One of the most productive areas for birding in Ridley Creek State Park is along Sycamore Mills Road adjoining Ridley Creek, with a short excursion up Forge Road. This route is shared with cyclists, fishermen, and hikers, and traverses several different habitats in less than one mile. The diversity of habitats accounts for the great variety of species seen. A several-hour walk during the spring and fall migrations might yield up to twenty-five species of warblers, six species of vireos, six species of thrushes, and several species each of flycatchers, woodpeckers, swallows, wrens, orioles, finches, and sparrows. The first three weeks in May and late August through September are the best times, as fantastic numbers of migrants are then funneling through the park. But every season has its attractions, making a birding trip worthwhile any time of the year. Many typical eastern landbirds nest at Ridley Creek State Park and nearby Tyler Arboretum (these are designated † after the species). More than a few types that regularly breed there are uncommon elsewhere in the Delaware Valley region.

Over twenty species of warblers are commonly seen along this route during migration: Black-and-white,† Blue-winged,† Northern Parula,† Yellow,† Magnolia, Black-throated Blue, Yellow-rumped (Myrtle), Black-throated Green, Cerulean,† Blackburnian, Chestnut-sided,† Bay-breasted, Blackpoll, Prairie,† Palm (mid- to late April), Ovenbird,† Northern and Louisiana† Water-thrushes, Kentucky,† Common Yellowthroat,† Yellow-breasted Chat,† Canada Warbler, and American Redstart.† Worm-eating,† Tennessee, Nashville, Pine (in April), and Wilson's Warblers are less frequently observed. Prothonotary, Golden-winged, Yellow-throated,† Connecticut, Mourning, and Hooded† Warblers have also been reported, albeit rarely. At least sixteen species of warblers have nested at Ridley Creek and Tyler Arboretum over the years, and fourteen of them are regular breeders, many choosing sights along Sycamore Mills Road and Forge Road.

All six species of eastern vireos may be seen during migration. The White-eyed,† Yellow-throated,† and Red-eyed† Vireos remain to nest along the above route, while the Warbling Vireo† favors several other locations in the area. The Solitary Vireo and (rarely) the Philadelphia Vireo pass through during the spring and fall waves.

Six species of thrushes are regularly seen during migration: American Robin,† Wood,† Hermit (in April), Swainson's (Olive-backed), and Gray-cheeked Thrushes, and Veery.† American Robin,† Wood Thrush,† and Veery† stay on to breed and are common throughout the summer. The Hermit Thrush is frequently observed during the winter and is the only thrush (other than wintering Robins and Eastern Bluebirds) to be expected during the colder months. The Swainson's Thrush is abundant both spring and fall, while the Gray-cheeked Thrush seems most common in May.

Many other landbirds are to be expected during the spring and fall migrations, and many remain to nest in the general area. Ring-necked Pheasant,† Mourning Dove,† Chimney Swift,† Ruby-throated Hummingbird,† Belted Kingfisher,† Common

(Yellow-shafted) Flicker,† Red-bellied,† Hairy,† and Downy† Woodpeckers, Eastern Kingbird,† Great Crested Flycatcher,† Eastern Phoebe,† Acadian Flycatcher,† Eastern (Wood) Pewee,† Tree,† Rough-winged (formerly nested), and Barn† Swallows, Blue Jay,† American (Common) Crow,† Black-capped and Carolina† Chickadees, Tufted Titmouse,† White-breasted Nuthatch,† House† and Carolina† Wrens, Northern Mockingbird,† Gray Catbird,† Brown Thrasher,† Blue-gray Gnatcatcher,† Golden-crowned and Ruby-crowned Kinglets (in April), Cedar Waxwing,† European Starling,† House Sparrow,† Eastern Meadowlark,† Red-winged Blackbird,† Orchard† and Northern (Baltimore)† Orioles, Common Grackle,† Scarlet Tanager,† Northern Cardinal,† Rose-breasted Grosbeak, Indigo Bunting,† Purple Finch (in April), American Goldfinch,† Rufous-sided Towhee,† Dark-eyed (Slate-colored) Junco (April), and Field,† White-throated (late April), Swamp,† and Song† Sparrows are commonly seen on a May trip. Broad-winged Hawk,† American Kestrel† (Sparrow Hawk), American Woodcock,† Yellow-billed† and Black-billed† Cuckoos, Common Nighthawk, Pileated Woodpecker,† Yellow-bellied Sapsucker (in April), Least and (in September) Olive-sided Flycatchers, Purple Martin, Brown-headed Cowbird,† House Finch,† and Chipping Sparrow† have also been observed along this route during migration, but much less frequently.

Over seventy-five species of landbirds are to be expected on a regular basis along Sycamore Mills and Forge Roads during the peak migration periods. Not all of these will be seen on any one trip, but you should easily observe fifty or more species by carefully working this route for several hours during the first three weeks in May.

To illustrate the birding potential of the park's varied habitats, we'll retrace our usual walk along Sycamore Mills and Forge Roads. After crossing the Sycamore Mills Bridge at the junction of Bishop Hollow Road (Ridley Creek Road) and Chapel Hill Road, you can park immediately to the right in a twelve-car earthen lot, or go seventy yards to the left along Barren Road to a smaller, six-car, lot. Begin in this latter area and search the crowded foliage along the stream's banks—this is a hot spot during spring migration. The Acadian Flycatcher† frequently nests in the tree branches overhanging the creek, as does the Blue-gray Gnatcatcher.† The Northern Parula Warbler† favors the draping vines, and an occasional pair may remain to breed. During the second week in May, listen for the distinctive notes of the Cerulean Warbler† and then scan the treetops for this elusive bird. Several pairs have nested here and around the first parking lot in a loose colony for many years.

Briefly walk the stream-side trail leading off to the right of the lot for forty yards to where the creek loops away from Barren Road. The forest canopy along the trail opens up into scattered groves of second growth and thickets. The Winter Wren is regularly observed working the tangles during the colder months up until mid-April. In May, the Belted Kingfisher† and Rough-winged Swallow† are frequently seen patrolling this loop, and may occasionally nest in the stream's earthen banks if they are not disturbed by fishermen. Blue-winged,† Yellow,† and Chestnut-sided† Warblers, Common Yellowthroat,† Indigo Bunting,† and American Goldfinch† can be found in the more open sections. In June 1972, we discovered a probable breeding pair of Yellow-throated Warblers that seemed to prefer the sycamore stand on the opposite bank of the creek (another pair was present nearby during the summer of 1979). Scan these trees; Orchard† and Baltimore† Orioles and Red-eyed Vireo† frequently nest here. Head back to the parking lot and be ready for the House† and Carolina† Wrens and American Redstart†—they are often heard defending their territories within earshot of this trail.

Stay close to the guard rail along Barren Road for the seventy-yard jaunt back to the first parking lot. The trees along the ridge behind the house and the towering, vine-draped pines next to the house attract hordes of migrating warblers. The Ruby-throated Hummingbird† is usually seen in this general area in May. The Yellow-throated Vireo,† frequently observed between here and the dam upstream, often nests in the large sycamore trees lining the creek. Listen for the Cerulean Warbler.†

Pass under the gate by the first parking lot and begin walking along Sycamore Mills Road. This road was closed to auto traffic when the area became a state park and now is used only by cyclists and fishermen. For the next 150 yards sycamores line the stream immediately to the right of Sycamore Mills Road, and the dark hardwood forest creeps up to the edge of the road on your left. A boulder dam then interrupts Ridley Creek; Cedar Waxwings† flood this area during their fall migration (late August through September), hawking the insects that gather at the dam. Immediately above the dam is a swampy section lined with willows. Yellow Warblers† and a pair of Canada Geese† can be found here, and Spotted and Solitary Sandpipers are occasionally seen working the muddy edges during May. Mallards† and Wood Ducks† are sometimes seen as they wing by, looking for an undisturbed pool.

Sycamore Mills Road parallels Ridley Creek for another seventy yards until Forge Road leads off to the left up a wooded hillside. Check the treetops around the burned-out colonial house for the Cerulean Warbler,† which particularly favors this location. Continue up Forge Road as it winds away from the creek and passes through several different habitats. For the first 200 yards, Forge Road climbs a fairly steep grade and is shaded by a deciduous forest typical of the eastern United States. The Ovenbird† is to be counted on here during the warmer months, while the "wood-chippy" trill of the Worm-eating Warbler† is occasionally heard in May. The Black-and-white Warbler† abounds during migration, and a few pairs may stay on to nest in this general area. Forge Road is one of the best locales to see all the migrating thrushes as well as the summering Wood Thrush† and Veery.† Red-bellied,† Hairy,† and Downy† Woodpeckers breed in these woods, as do the Blue-gray Gnatcatcher,† Tufted Titmouse,† and Carolina Chickadee.† The Yellow-bellied Sapsucker, White-breasted Nuthatch,† and Brown Creeper are regularly observed October through April, while the Pileated Woodpecker† has been reported at various times of the year, albeit rarely.

Forge Road then bears to the left, crosses a small running spring, and leaves the dark woodland behind. For the next hundred yards, conifers border the left side. Look for the Red-breasted Nuthatch and winter finches during the coldest months. Moist, dense thickets planted with intermediate-height trees line the right side of the road. Breeding Chestnut-sided Warbler† and American Redstart† work the middle story of these trees, while the White-eyed Vireo† and Common Yellowthroat† call from the thickets below. This stretch is particularly good for migrating warblers.

A narrow road then leads off to the right toward a group of colo-

nial buildings that serve as a residence for park personnel. Immediately past this road and to the right of Forge Road is a vast expanse
of brushy meadows and thickets dotted with islands of second
growth. Nesting Blue-winged† and Prairie† Warblers and Yellow-
breasted Chat† are found here along with Indigo Bunting,† American Goldfinch,† and Field Sparrow.† During late March, American
Woodcock† can often be seen displaying in this area. Continue
up Forge Road for another hundred yards to a second open area
(picnic area 17); the same birds can be seen here also.

At this point, we usually head back down Forge Road toward
the car. You can continue westward along Forge Road (which
serves as the southern border of the park) for approximately one
mile until it meets Painter Road at the northwest corner of Tyler
Arboretum. This route traverses small woodlots alternating with
scrubby fields and is relatively quiet. During the fall and winter
various birds of prey frequent this area. Turkey Vulture, Sharp-
shinned and Red-tailed Hawks, American Kestrel,† and an occasional Northern Harrier (Marsh Hawk) are seen. Slate-colored
Junco and American Tree, Field,† White-throated, Fox, and Song†
Sparrows work the hedgerows and wood borders. Wintering Common Redpoll and White-crowned and Swamp† Sparrows are sometimes discovered along these protective strips. Eastern Bluebirds†
are commonly found along Forge Road in the northwest portion
of the Arboretum and are especially noticeable during the colder
months.

Back at the junction of Forge and Sycamore Mills Roads, walk
north along Sycamore Mills Road for approximately one and one-
half miles to the youth hostel, if you have the time. Ridley Creek
hugs the road along this stretch and the habitat consists of a clear
moving stream lined with brushy tangles and shaded by a canopy
of various hardwoods (sycamore, beech, maple, oak, hickory, and
tulip poplar predominate). Assorted warblers, vireos, and thrushes
are seen during migration. Beginning in mid-April, Northern and
Louisiana† Waterthrushes and the Swamp Sparrow† are frequently
observed working the creek. Fair numbers of the Louisiana Water-
thrush† remain to nest along the undisturbed portions of the stream.
The flycatcher family is well represented here. Eastern Kingbird,†
Great Crested Flycatcher,† Eastern Phoebe,† Acadian Flycatcher,† and Eastern Pewee† are common during the warmer months.

For the past several years, the Least Flycatcher has summered below the youth hostel where Sycamore Mills Road veers away from Ridley Creek. The Willow ("Fitz-Bew") Flycatcher† has also been recorded here during the summer. The sycamore-lined dirt road leading to the youth hostel from Sycamore Mills Road is good for Yellow Warbler,† Baltimore Oriole,† and Brown-headed Cowbird.† Be on the lookout for Warbling Vireo† and Orchard Oriole,† which occasionally nest here. Walk the nearby white-blazed trail back toward Forge Road. Some years, the Hooded Warbler† nests near the rocky bluffs guarding this trail.

If time is limited to several hours, the route we've outlined affords the most birds in the least time. But many more birds have been seen in the general area, and there are other productive areas within Ridley Creek State Park and Tyler Arboretum. These spots are mentioned because they too host large numbers of birds or because certain desirable species may be seen here more reliably than elsewhere.

The Colonial Pennsylvania Plantation within the state park is a living museum of a 1776 Delaware County farm. After entering the park's main entrance off Route 3 (West Chester Pike), drive 1.3 miles along Sandy Flash Drive North to the plantation. Walking the dirt road and wooden bridge across the creek below the farmhouse can be very productive. Acadian Flycatcher,† Warbling Vireo,† and Orchard Oriole† are frequently seen here, along with many other species. An admission fee is charged, but it's worthwhile as the public may observe and participate in authentic colonial farming scenes.

The park office is located in "Hunting Hill," the former Jeffords mansion, which was constructed in 1914 around a small stone farmhouse that forms the core of the park office and now serves as a reception center. After entering the park's main entrance off of Route 3 (West Chester Pike), drive 3 miles along Sandy Flash Drive North, Gradyville Road, and Sandy Flash Drive South to the headquarters. Formal gardens, deciduous woodlands, and an old orchard surround the park office. Yellow-billed† and Black-billed† Cuckoos, Acadian Flycatcher,† Yellow-breasted Chat,† and Orchard Oriole† commonly breed in the immediate area. On the way to the park office, stop by the bridle path crossing Gradyville Road and walk this dirt trail as it hugs Ridley Creek. For the past several years the Least Flycatcher has summered here. The swampy thickets to the left of the path are ideal habitat for Willow Flycatcher,† which has nested here and at several other locations throughout the park.

A gigantic sycamore tree hulking over a one-lane bridge across Ridley Creek (at the junction of Rose Tree Road and Ridley Creek Road) provides another birding attraction. Eastern Kingbird,† Warbling Vireo,† and Orchard Oriole† use this favorite tree every year, and all three can easily be observed from Rose Tree Road. This section, which is outside the park boundaries, is fairly extensive and used only by fishermen.

Walk the stream-side trails above and below the bridge. Upstream is lined with sycamores, which should be screened for members of the vireo and oriole families. Downstream is edged with briers and splashes of wildflowers, including at least five color variations of Spiderwort. Behind and to the right of the Spiderworts is a small cattail swamp dotted with dead trees. Yellow Warbler† and Red-winged Blackbird† breed here. A pair of Wood Ducks† have nested in holes in the tree trunks for the past several years. Vast areas of open brush mixed with stands of second growth are encountered along both sides of Rose Tree Road approaching the bridge. Tree† and Barn† Swallows quarter the fields from above. Yellow† and Prairie† Warblers, Common Yellowthroat,† Indigo Bunting,† American Goldfinch,† and Field† and Song† Sparrows use this locale for nesting.

To reach this area, cross the Sycamore Mills Bridge and turn left onto Barren Road. Travel 1.2 miles to Painter Road and make another left (Tyler Arboretum is to the right). Drive 0.7 miles to Rose Tree Road and make a left at the stop sign. Continue another 0.45 miles along Rose Tree Road to a small gravel parking lot at Ridley Creek Road just beyond the one-lane bridge. After birding, turn left onto Ridley Creek Road and drive 1.6 miles back to Sycamore Mills Bridge.

Tyler Arboretum

Tyler (Painter) Arboretum covers 700 acres and shares a boundary (Forge Road) with Ridley Creek State Park. The Arboretum contains a wealth of both formal and informal plant collections. Most of the eastern United States' native trees and wildflowers can be found here. Tyler Arboretum has extensive trails for hiking and birding. A detailed map of the various trails and plantings can be obtained at the visitors' center next to Lachford Hall.

From Sycamore Mills Bridge, drive 1.2 miles along Barren Road to Painter Road. Turn right onto Painter Road and travel another 0.95 miles to the Arboretum's parking lot on your right. Follow the signs for the short walk to the headquarters.

The most productive time to visit Tyler Arboretum is during the first three weeks in May. After birding Ridley Creek in the morning, spend an hour or two at Tyler. This will add up to a dozen species not usually encountered along Ridley Creek. In addition, you will be treated to a display of various trees and shrubs. From the visitors' center, walk down the hill across a small wooden bridge along the Minshall Painter Trail (Painter Brothers Trail). This trail passes a small pond and then winds up a steep hill for approximately three hundred yards through the famous rhododendron collection. The large deciduous woodland to the left of the rhododendrons is excellent for migrating and nesting flycatchers, vireos, and warblers. To the right is the Pinetum and a vast expanse of both mowed and uncut meadows dotted with dogwoods, conifers, and large shade trees. The Pine Warbler is occasionally seen migrating through the Pinetum in April. Brown Thrasher,† Rufous-sided Towhee,† and Field† and Song† Sparrows breed in the more scrubby unmowed areas, while the Eastern Kingbird† and Chipping Sparrow† sing from the treetops in May. The Eastern Bluebird† uses the numerous green nesting boxes and can frequently be seen working the nearby dogwoods. During the colder months, Eastern Bluebird† and Purple Finch can be found along the wooded edges.

Minshall Painter Trail turns left after leaving the rhododendrons. Follow the trail for several hundred yards toward the formal dogwood planting. The Eastern Meadowlark† calls from the fields to the right of the trail during May, while Tree† and Barn† Swallows hawk insects overhead. Breeding Indigo Bunting† and American Goldfinch† favor the nearby scrubby thickets. The trail continues past the dogwoods for another hundred yards or so and leads into a large wooded ravine. The woods behind the dogwoods should be checked for the Great Horned Owl† throughout the year. Continue down the Minshall Painter Trail for about sixty yards into the ravine. At the second crosstrail, listen for the resident breeding Kentucky Warbler.† The surrounding deciduous woodlands are good for nesting Great Crested† and Acadian† Flycatchers, Eastern Pewee,† Wood Thrush,† Veery,† Blue-gray Gnatcatcher,† Red-eyed Vireo,† Ovenbird,† American Redstart,† Baltimore Oriole,† and an occasional Scarlet Tanager.†

The Dismal Run Trail parallels the very small Dismal Run Creek, which wanders through the valley below Barren Road. Turn right onto Painter Road from Barren Road and drive one-quarter of a mile to the trail entrance on your right. The stream is fed by many springs coursing down the wooded hillsides as it winds along the bottom of the ravine. This is one of the most reliable places to see the Winter Wren and Hermit Thrush from fall through early spring. This walk is also rewarding during the landbird migration beginning in late April. Among the warblers, Louisiana Waterthrush† and Kentucky Warbler† are commonly seen and remain to nest. The rarely seen Hooded Warbler† should also be looked for here and in the East Woods, located on the other side of Barren Road.

Back at the headquarters, check the various feeders for wintering finches and sparrows during the colder months (November through early April). Slate-colored Junco, American Tree, Field,† White-throated, and Song† Sparrows, and an occasional Fox Sparrow frequent the shrubbery guarding the well-stocked feeders. Both Chickadees (the Black-capped is the commoner species in winter), Tufted Titmouse,† Northern Cardinal,† Purple and House† Finches, and American Goldfinch† make numerous forays for seeds. Search the evergreen shrubs and tall conifers around the visitors' center and parking lot for White-breasted† and Red-breasted Nuthatches, Brown Creeper, Golden-crowned and Ruby-crowned Kinglets, Purple Finch, and an occasional Pine Siskin. This area is one of the better spots in the Delaware Valley region for the wintering Red-breasted Nuthatch. During invasion years Red and White-winged Crossbills and the Evening Grosbeak can sometimes be found near these evergreen stands.

Finally, an "owl prowl" is sponsored by the Arboretum in early March. Good numbers of Common Screech† and Great Horned† Owls are seen (or heard). Some years, Barn, Long-eared, and Saw-whet Owls are recorded. Be sure to call for reservations several weeks in advance, as this trip fills up early.

Springton Reservoir

Springton Reservoir is a large man-made impoundment that supplies much of the water for Delaware County, Pennsylvania. It is reached along the same route to Sycamore Mills Bridge.

After turning left onto Bishop Hollow Road from Route 3 (West Chester Pike), drive 1.8 miles to the first stop sign at Gradyville Road. Turn right onto Gradyville Road and travel another hundred yards or so to a large parking lot on your left.

Hike the lakeside trail around to the right, cross Gradyville Road and Bridge, and continue to walk into the woods along the trail to the right of the reservoir until you reach Crum Creek. In mid-August, when much of the reservoir is drawn down, Killdeer† and Spotted Sandpiper are common on the exposed mudflats. Several species of sandpipers (usually the Western, Semipalmated, and Solitary Sandpipers) are occasionally seen during their fall migration (August). Earlier in the summer, breeding Mallard† and Wood Duck,† along with the Green Heron,† frequent the Crum Creek area. In past years the Pine Warbler† has nested in the large evergreen stands bordering the reservoir. Colder weather brings an assortment of waterfowl, including Canada Goose,† Mallard,† American Black Duck, Ring-necked Duck, Greater and Lesser Scaup, American Coot, and other species. These birds are best observed near the Route 252 dam.

For more information, and the Arboretum birdlist, write:

The John J. Tyler Arboretum
Box 216
515 Painter Road
Lima, Pa. 19037
Phone: (215) 566-5431
        (215) L06-9133

The staffed visitors' center is open daily.

For information, and the Ridley Creek birdlist, write:

Ridley Creek State Park
Sycamore Mills Road
Route 36
Media, Pa. 19063
Phone: (215) 566-4800

Directions to Ridley Creek State Park

From the City Line Avenue Exit of the Schuylkill Expressway (Interstate 76), continue for 5.2 miles along U.S. 1 South
to the intersection with Route 3 (West Chester Pike). Make a
right onto Route 3 West and drive 5.8 miles to the intersection
with Route 252 in Newtown Square. Proceed through this light
on Route 3 West to the next light (0.1 miles further). Turn left
onto Bishop Hollow Road and travel 3.3 miles to Chapel Hill
Road (passing the intersections with Gradyville Road and
Providence Road). Make a right onto Chapel Hill Road across
the narrow Sycamore Mills Bridge. Barren Road (to Tyler
Arboretum) is to the left and the Sycamore Mills Road birding
tour is immediately to the right. A one-way trip takes approximately one-half hour from the Schuylkill Expressway.

If the small parking lots next to the Sycamore Mills Bridge
are full, proceed to picnic area 17 in the state park proper.
Then walk down Forge Road to Sycamore Mills Road. The
main entrance to Ridley Creek State Park is reached by driving
3.3 miles along Route 3 West past the intersection with Route
252. Turn left onto the main park road (Sandy Flash Drive) and
travel 3 miles to the park office. To reach picnic area 17, take
the second left after the park office along Sandy Flash Drive
South (0.45 miles past the headquarters). Drive 0.9 miles along
this winding road to the large parking lot on Forge Road.

Map 2
Directions to Ridley Creek State Park

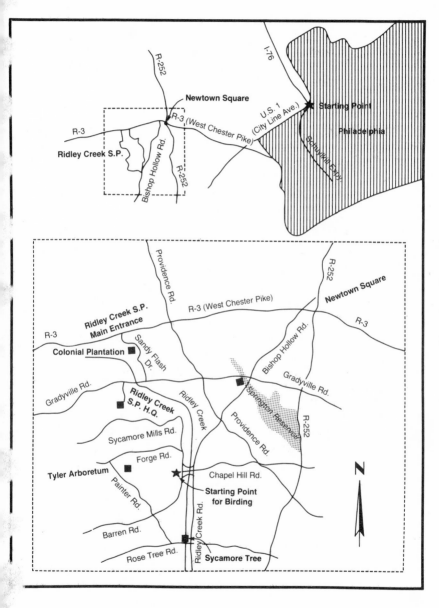

Map 3
Ridley Creek State Park

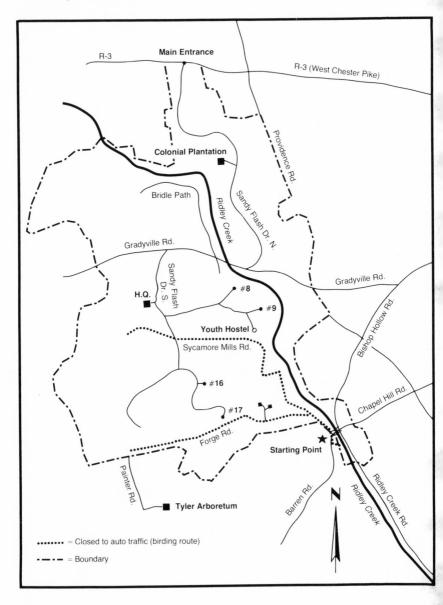

R-3

Main Entrance

R-3 (West Chester Pike)

Colonial Plantation

Providence Rd.

Bridle Path

Ridley Creek

Sandy Flash Dr. N.

Gradyville Rd.

Sandy Flash Dr. S.

Gradyville Rd.

#8

H.Q.

#9

Bishop Hollow Rd.

Youth Hostel

Sycamore Mills Rd.

#16

Chapel Hill Rd.

#17

Forge Rd.

Starting Point

Painter Rd.

Barren Rd.

Tyler Arboretum

Ridley Creek Rd.

Ridley Creek

N

•••••••• = Closed to auto traffic (birding route)

— · — · — = Boundary

Map 4
Tyler Arboretum

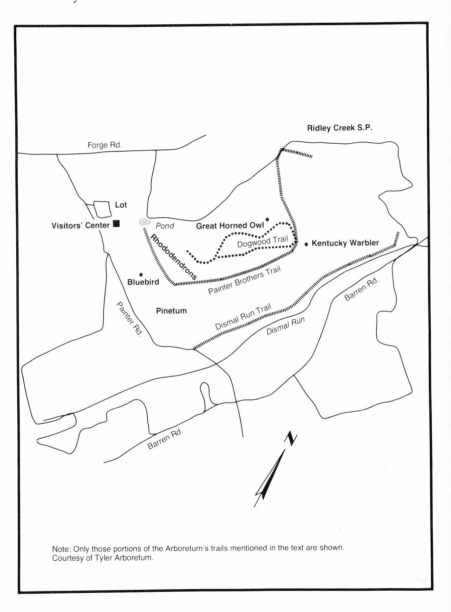

Note: Only those portions of the Arboretum's trails mentioned in the text are shown.
Courtesy of Tyler Arboretum.

Tinicum National Environmental Center and Philadelphia International Airport, Pennsylvania

Tinicum National Environmental Center

Congress officially established Tinicum as a National Environmental Center in 1972 to preserve the last remaining fresh-water tidal marsh along the Delaware River. Between 1955 and 1972, the refuge (which constituted 600 acres in 1978) was managed by the Philadelphia Department of Recreation. Located in extreme southwestern Philadelphia, the preserve is surrounded by industrial complexes and housing developments, and is within two miles of Philadelphia International Airport.

Tinicum's main attraction is a large fresh-water impoundment straddling tidal Darby Creek, which serves as its western boundary. To date, over 271 species have been identified on the refuge—including many types not usually seen in eastern Pennsylvania. Large numbers of waterfowl and shorebirds visit Tinicum during their spring and fall migrations. Many species (designated † after the name) remain to breed in the area. If you are planning a Big Day in southeastern Pennsylvania, then Tinicum is a must during early May. Only forty minutes' drive from Ridley Creek State Park, Tinicum's waterbirds complement the landbirds seen earlier in the day at Ridley Creek.

Tinicum's principal habitat is a fresh-water marsh, the depth of which is controlled by rainfall and by adjustable flow gates to Darby Creek. When water levels are high, the impoundment is more of a shallow lake, dotted with tiny islands and encroaching vegetation, which provide nesting sites for various birds. When water levels are lower, especially in the late summer, the marsh consists of extensive mudflats guarding isolated potholes, thus setting the stage for large concentrations of migrating shorebirds, including some of the rarer species.

A gravel dike that separates the marsh from Darby Creek serves as the main vantage point for birding the refuge. This one-lane road (closed to cars) begins at the visitors' center and snakes around the western boundary of the preserve for approximately one and one-half miles. The dike itself is flanked by narrow strips of vegetation. The scattered trees, predominantly willows, are of the intermediate-height range. Stands of cattails and rushes, along with a carpet of typical fresh-water marsh plants, edge the banks.

Darby Creek forms the western border of the refuge. Its slow, dark waters, so vulnerable to the nearby industries, rise and fall with the tide. Vast stretches of marsh are bathed by its reaches. During low tide, expansive mudflats are exposed, attracting migrating shorebirds. The flats at the end of the dike road (one and one-half miles) are especially good if water levels in the impoundment are high.

Meadows, dotted with thickets and islands of second-growth woodland, serve as the marsh's eastern boundary. Housing developments are rapidly gouging into this buffer zone. A service road meanders through this section and finally leads into a thick woodland that separates the southern part of the marsh from nearby Bartram Avenue. This area hosts many of the landbirds indigenous to the refuge.

As stated before, the dike road is Tinicum's main birding route. Halfway along the dike a steel platform juts out into the marsh, affording a panoramic view of the preserve's waterbirds. A zoom scope allows effortless observation of the sometimes distant birds, cutting down on hiking time.

In 1978, a Master Plan for the development and administration of the Tinicum National Environmental Center was drawn up under the supervision of the U.S. Fish and Wildlife Service. Further land acquisition, wetland reclamation, and habitat modification have been proposed for the center. Birding should generally improve as a result of this, although certain species may relocate depending on the changes in their local environment.

Tinicum offers a unique potpourri of birds, depending on the time of year. Although the spring and fall migrations account for the greatest number of species, each season provides attractions to make a birding trip worthwhile. The refuge's waterfowl and marshbirds serve as the magnet and swell any birder's tri-state list. With a few notable exceptions, landbirds are not the main reason to visit

Tinicum, as most species can be seen more reliably elsewhere, for example at Ridley Creek. Stop by Tinicum's visitors' center and ask Jim Carroll "what's in town." He pointed out many of our "lifers" over fifteen years ago.

Spring begins in mid-March. Wintering ducks are joined by large numbers of migrating waterfowl that use the refuge as a staging area. Pied-billed Grebe,† Canada Goose,† Mallard,† American Black Duck,† Gadwall, Common Pintail,† Green-winged† and Blue-winged† Teals, American Wigeon, Northern Shoveler,† Greater and Lesser Scaup, Ruddy Duck, and American Coot† are certain to be seen. Also, but less frequently, seen are Ring-necked Duck and Hooded and Common Mergansers. Horned Grebe, Whistling Swan, Wood Duck,† Canvasback, Common Goldeneye, Bufflehead, and (rarely) the Redhead occasionally visit during their spring migration. Tinicum is one of more reliable locations in the Delaware Valley for Ring-necked Duck and Lesser Scaup. Patiently scoping the marsh from the platform is the best way to see the ducks.

As the waterfowl slowly thin out during April, herons and egrets begin to invade the refuge. Great Blue Herons that remained the winter are joined by fair numbers of Green Heron† (favors Darby Creek), Great (Common) Egret, and Black-crowned Night Heron.† Snowy Egret, Little Blue Heron, Cattle Egret, Louisiana Heron, and Glossy Ibis are occasionally seen during the warmer months. The Yellow-crowned Night Heron† is a rare visitor to Tinicum, although a breeding pair was present in 1977.

Least† and American† Bitterns begin to select their nesting sites in late April. Although common, the bitterns' secretiveness makes them appear much rarer. King† and Virginia† Rails and Sora† are common spring migrants, and a few pairs may remain to breed. Unless you actively search among the reeds, they are likely to be missed. Common Gallinule† and American Coot† present no such problem—they are easily noticed.

Early May heralds the shorebird migration. Semipalmated Plover, Killdeer,† American Woodcock† (arrives in March), Common Snipe, Spotted Sandpiper,† Greater and Lesser Yellowlegs, and Least and Semipalmated Sandpipers are common. Solitary and Pectoral Sandpipers, Dunlin, and Short-billed Dowitcher occur less frequently. Tinicum is one of the best locales in the tri-state region to observe the Solitary Sandpiper during spring migration.

Late summer promises more species and greater concentrations of shorebirds, perhaps because the mudflats are more extensive at that time. The various marsh- and shorebirds are best observed by periodically stopping along the dike and glassing the nearby water's edge.

Early May also signals the major landbird movement. Many of the species seen at Ridley Creek are encountered here too, although usually in far smaller numbers. Many of the migrants can be found working the brush and trees along the dike. Certain birds associated with an open-marsh habitat are expected at Tinicum. The ones that remain to breed will be discussed later.

All the swallows, except perhaps the Cliff Swallow, frequent the refuge during their spring trek. In early May, Tinicum is one of the most reliable spots in the area to see the Bank and Rough-winged Swallows. Yellow,† Cape May, Palm (April), Mourning, and Wilson's Warblers, and Northern Waterthrush seem more regular here than elsewhere in southeastern Pennsylvania, although the Mourning and Wilson's are by no means common. Of the spring transients, Black-and-white, Yellow,† and Yellow-rumped (Myrtle) Warblers, Northern Waterthrush, Common Yellowthroat,† and American Redstart† are the most common. Various members of the blackbird family are also present, including Red-winged† and Rusty Blackbirds, Common Grackle,† and Brown-headed Cowbird.†

The sparrow family is still well represented in early May, as many species winter over. Savannah,† American Tree (April), Field,† White-throated, Fox (early April), Swamp,† and Song† Sparrows are common, with Vesper, Chipping, and White-crowned Sparrows less so. Most of the sparrows are more conspicuous during the colder months, when vegetation is less thick and there are fewer competing birds.

June signals the beginning of the summer season at Tinicum. Over seventy-five species have been recorded as nesting on the refuge. The mosquitoes are generally tolerable during the day, and the sight of duck broods on the impoundment can be rewarding. But most birders visit Tinicum during the summer to observe its various "specialty" birds.

As mentioned before, Least† and American† Bitterns nest in the reeds edging the marsh, but are difficult to glimpse. King† and

Virginia† Rails and Sora,† although official breeders, require even more sleuthing and luck to find.

The Northern Harrier† (Marsh Hawk) has nested at Tinicum, but its present status as a breeding bird is uncertain. This species is more likely seen quartering the marsh during the other seasons. The American Kestrel† (Sparrow Hawk) is the other breeding raptor at the preserve.

The nesting Empidonax at Tinicum is the Traill's Flycatcher, which is now considered two separate species, the Willow ("Fitz-Bew") and the Alder ("Fee-Bee'-o"). Although the refuge list notes just the opposite, the Willow Flycatcher† is the more common, and is frequently seen working the shrubs along the dike. It favors singing from the old telephone wires near the platform. Walking the service road is another good way to tally this species.

Both Fish† and American† (Common) Crows frequent the refuge at all seasons. Their calls are the only reliable way to distinguish them. They seem most common when water levels are low, especially if dead carp litter the flats.

House,† Carolina,† and Marsh† (Long-billed Marsh) Wrens nest in the preserve. Visit Tinicum to observe the Marsh Wren,† which favors the reeds and cattail stands along the dike. Its characteristic song and flight pattern alert the birder long before its features can be distinguished.

Some years, Warbling Vireo† and Orchard Oriole† nest in the taller shade trees lining the dike and the service road. Check the trees by the water control gates near the platform, as this is a favorite location for the Warbling Vireo.† The service road along the eastern border of the refuge passes through ideal habitat for Blue Grosbeak†; a breeding pair was present in 1978, in addition to the perennial pair that nests behind the airport. Red-winged Blackbird,† Indigo Bunting,† and American Goldfinch† are common breeders, while the nesting Swamp Sparrow† is more likely seen at Tinicum than elsewhere in the region.

Fall migration starts in August, when shorebirds return to Tinicum on their way south. Drier summers produce extensive mudflats, which attract large numbers of birds, including some uncommon species. The spring transients are more plentiful now, and Black-bellied Plover, Stilt and Western Sandpipers, and an occasional Sanderling also visit the August flats. Be on the lookout for "exotic" migrants. Lesser (American) Golden Plover (early September), Hudsonian Godwit, Ruff, and Wilson's and Northern Phalaropes occur almost annually, especially if water levels are down. Don't expect to see these birds on a random visit, but repeated coverage over a number of years from August through mid-September should produce these "lifers," as well as even rarer species. The Common Snipe increases in numbers as the fall progresses; many remain through the colder months.

Various terns, including Forster's, Caspian, and Black Terns, sporadically visit Tinicum during August and September.

Labor Day coincides with the fall warbler peak. Twenty species are listed as common. Cape May, Connecticut, and Mourning (very rare) Warblers are more regular at Tinicum than elsewhere in eastern Pennsylvania, especially during the fall. The tree groves lining the creek next to the platform are favorite resting and feeding sites during migration. Bobolinks are especially common from late August through September among the reeds adjoining the dike road. Their drab yellow plumage distinguishes them from the rustier-colored Rusty Blackbirds, which generally arrive later in the season.

Fall blends imperceptibly into winter during November. Waterfowl, which started arriving in October, now cover the refuge's open water in unbelievable concentrations. All the species listed as spring migrants or nesters are more plentiful during the fall and early winter. Canvasback, Bufflehead, and Hooded Merganser are likely now, and the Redhead is reported practically every year. Search among the vast floats of Green-winged Teal† for the Common (European) race—individuals are spotted every fall. Many of the ducks stay the winter if ice doesn't choke off the open water.

Hawks and owls start to build up during late November, using Tinicum for their wintering quarters. Red-tailed Hawk, Northern Harrier,† and American Kestrel† are certain to be seen from the dike. The Rough-legged Hawk also winters at the preserve, although in much smaller numbers. These birds are most frequently seen working the tidal marshes of Darby Creek and behind the airport.

The Short-eared Owl† is another specialty of Tinicum. They are best observed by combing the meadows along the refuge's eastern border until one of these large moth-like birds springs into the air. While working this area, stop by the scattered tree stands that dot the meadows. Wintering owls frequently roost here; Common Screech† and Long-eared Owls are reported more often than Barn† and Saw-whet Owls.

Gulls are most common from November through early December. Greater Black-backed, Herring, and Ring-billed Gulls frequent the marsh's numerous islands, especially after dry summers when carp are beached on the flats. The Laughing Gull visits occasionally during warm weather, but is very rare during the winter. The Glaucous and Bonaparte's Gulls visit the refuge annually in very small numbers during the colder months, but seem most likely closer to the river.

Search the trees surrounding the visitors' center and along the dike for the Loggerhead Shrike. This bird is seen practically every year between September and March.

The sparrow family sports more members than most other groups from mid-October through April. A walk along the dike produces Savannah,† Swamp,† and Song† Sparrows among the reeds and marsh grass. Dark-eyed (Slate-colored) Junco and White-throated and Fox Sparrows work the leafy bottoms of the dense thickets, especially near the platform. The trail through the meadows and briers along the eastern border of the marsh is a favorite for American Tree, Field,† and White-crowned Sparrows. Tinicum is one of the better spots in the region to see the White-crowned Sparrow during the colder months. "Psshing" and "squeaking" quickly attracts hordes of wintering sparrows. Small numbers of Winter Wren are also recorded during the winter season at Tinicum.

The barren field between the entrance to the refuge and the parking lot by the headquarters occasionally hosts small flocks of Horned Lark and Snow Bunting, plus an infrequent Lapland Longspur. These winter birds range widely between the refuge and the more expansive grounds of the airport.

The Delaware River

The Delaware River near the Westinghouse complex is a haven for waterfowl during the colder months.

After leaving the refuge, turn right onto 84th Avenue for 0.65 miles. Make a right at the second light onto Bartram Avenue and continue 1.6 miles to the next light. Bear right onto

Route 291 West and travel 1.2 miles to 4th Avenue in the town of Essington. Turn left onto 4th Avenue and go another 0.5 miles to the intersection with Tinicum Island Avenue (dead end). Bear right past the stop sign for 0.2 miles and park in a small earthen lot to the left of the road.

Lock your car and walk the railroad tracks, which wind through a crowded stand of reeds for several hundred yards. Where the tracks bear sharply to the left, the Delaware River comes into view. Vast rafts of Ruddy and American Black† Ducks float between this point and an island in the middle of the river. All the ducks seen at Tinicum can be found here, and numbers of Whistling Swan and an occasional Red-necked Grebe also visit this stretch during the winter season. Various herons and egrets work the water's edge during the warmer months.

The reeds along the tracks that snake between the river and the airport are excellent habitat for the Northern Harrier† and Short-eared Owl.† Presumably both may still nest here, but they are most reliably seen from November through March. This area is rapidly shrinking due to encroachment by the nearby airport.

The Philadelphia International Airport is a vast expanse of marsh, cut meadows, and paved landing strips. Follow the same route from Tinicum to the Delaware River site. Turn left at the intersection of 4th Avenue and Tinicum Island Avenue. For the next mile or so between here and Cargo City there are several access points to the airport grounds off Tinicum Island Avenue. Most of this area is fenced in, but you can approach close enough to set up for birding. During early September, Upland Sandpiper (Plover), Buff-breasted Sandpiper (rare), and Lesser Golden and Black-bellied Plovers visit these flats on their way south. These same areas host Horned Lark, Water Pipit (October), Snow Bunting, and an occasional Lapland Longspur during the colder months. Northern Harrier,† Rough-legged Hawk, and Short-eared Owl† should be looked for in winter, as well as the Snowy Owl when it makes its cyclic invasions.

Behind the Airport

"Behind the airport" refers to a large area of varied habitats between the Philadelphia International Airport and the nearby Delaware River. Stands of cattails and phragmites, open fields, drainage ditches and marshes, isolated tree groves, and the Delaware River itself provide a rich opportunity to observe many local "specialties."

After leaving Tinicum, make a right onto 84th Avenue for 0.65 miles. At the second light turn left onto Bartram Avenue and, following the signs for Interstate 95 North, drive 0.3 miles to the next light. Make a right and travel 1 mile past Route 291 and past the Overseas Terminal to the fourth light. Continue straight through this busy intersection. Do not bear right for the loop to I-95 North. Drive 0.9 miles along the winding road through the reeds to the sign for Old Fort Mifflin. Bear right here, continuing on the main road for another 0.5 miles to a large field beside the ARCO tank farm (on the left). A boat-launching dock on the Delaware River is 0.6 miles further down the road.

During the winter, the area behind the airport is excellent for birds of prey. Northern Harrier,† Red-tailed Hawk, and American Kestrel† are seen practically every trip. This is one of the better spots in the Delaware Valley region to observe the Rough-legged Hawk and Short-eared Owl† as they patrol the fields and marshes adjoining the airport. Other birds, including the Sharp-shinned, Cooper's, and Red-shouldered Hawks, are occasionally seen during the colder months.

The large open field next to the ARCO tank farm should be checked for Horned Lark, Water Pipit, Snow Bunting, and an occasional Lapland Longspur.

During the warmer months, Willow Flycatcher,† Red-winged Blackbird,† Blue Grosbeak,† Indigo Bunting,† American Goldfinch,† and Swamp Sparrow† can be found nesting in their appropriate habitats. A pair of Blue Grosbeaks† favor the isolated tree groves bordering the fields and marshes along the main road. Various herons, egrets, bitterns, gulls, and terns are seen along the river itself.

Bear left at the sign for Old Fort Mifflin and follow the shabby road off to the left past sewage treatment ponds and landfill sites. This is a good area for shorebirds during the spring and fall migrations.

For more information, and the refuge birdlist, write:

Tinicum National Environmental
    Center
Center Headquarters
Suite 104, Scott Plaza 2
Philadelphia, Pa. 19113
Phone: (215) 521-0662

Tinicum National Environmental
    Center
Visitor Contact Station
86th Street and Lindbergh Blvd.
Philadelphia, Pa. 19153
Phone: (215) 365-3118

Directions to Tinicum National Environmental Center

From the City Line Avenue Exit of the Schuylkill Express-way (Interstate 76), drive 5.2 miles on U.S. 1 South (City Line Avenue) to the intersection with Route 3 (West Chester Pike). Pass through this intersection, and go another 0.1 miles to the next light. Make a left onto Lansdowne Avenue and drive 3.7 miles along Lansdowne Avenue to MacDade Blvd. Make a right onto MacDade Blvd., but stay in the left lane for 0.25 miles to the second light. Bear left onto Chester Pike and pro-ceed another 0.45 miles to Calcon Hook Road (second light). Make a left onto Calcon Hook Road and drive 0.9 miles to the next light, which is Hook Road. Turn left onto Hook Road, and loop around the oil tank farm. After 0.55 miles you will come to the Cobblestone Apartments at the next light. Make a right and continue for 0.2 miles to the Tinicum National Environmental Center on the right. Go through the gate and follow the gravel road for several hundred yards to the parking lot by the visi-tors' center. The dike road around the preserve begins just be-low here, but it is closed to auto traffic and must be walked.

An alternative route is via the Penrose Avenue Bridge, which is now called the George Platt Bridge. From the Schuylkill Expressway (Interstate 76) take Exit 5 for the Airport and 26th Street. At the second light make a right and cross the Penrose Avenue Bridge. Immediately after the bridge go 0.4 miles and, following the signs for I-95 South and Island Avenue, make a right. Travel another 0.4 miles to the next light and make a left onto Bartram Avenue (still following the signs for I-95 South). Drive 0.3 miles and make a right at the first light onto 84th Avenue. Continue 0.65 miles to the second light and make a left at the Cobblestone Apartments. The entrance to Tinicum is 0.2 miles further.

Map 5
Directions to Tinicum National Environmental Center

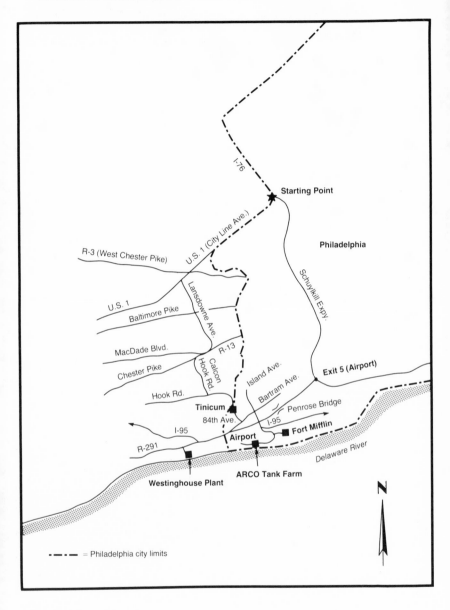

Map 6
Tinicum National Environmental Center

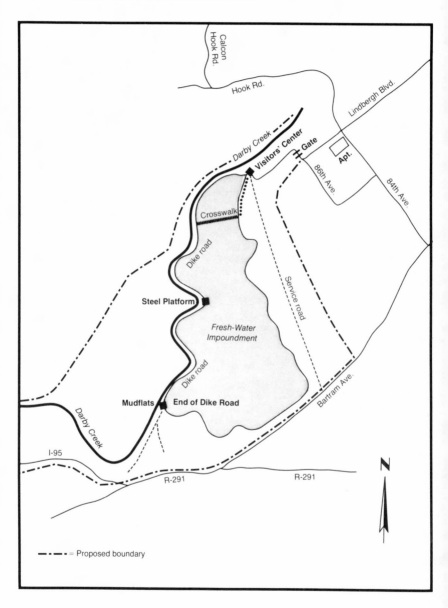

------ = Proposed boundary

Hawk Mountain Sanctuary and Bake Oven Knob, Pennsylvania

Hawk Mountain Sanctuary

On a few stony outcroppings of Tuscarora Sandstone, sitting atop a mountain ridge in eastern Pennsylvania, thousands of people gather each fall to watch a spectacle no one ever forgets. This is the hawk migration over Hawk Mountain Sanctuary. And those who do not come specifically to observe hawks come to sit peacefully, get caught up in the quiet but growing enthusiasm, and behold a seventy-mile panorama of mountains and valleys painted with fall's colors. The blazing October yellows, oranges, and reds of the dense oak and birch forest contrast with the darker shades of the scattered evergreens and the tawny browns of the valley fields.

Located roughly between the cities of Harrisburg and Allentown, a few miles from the village of Kempton, Hawk Mountain is just a dot on the Kittatinny Ridge. This "endless mountain" of the Lenape Indians rises in southeastern New York State and sprawls through five states to Virginia; it is the easternmost ridge of the Appalachian system and sits 1,520 feet above sea level.

Established in 1934 as a refuge from the hunters who climbed the mountain on windy fall days to gun down hundreds of migrating raptors, Hawk Mountain now covers over 2,000 acres of the surrounding mountainside. Two lookouts, North and South, provide easy viewing of the hawks. The South Lookout lies only 200 yards from the entrance, while the North is two-thirds of a mile further up a snaking trail. Through membership fees and a nominal charge to visitors ($1.00 for adults, 50¢ for children in 1979), many improvements have been made, including construction of a beautifully designed headquarters, which seconds as a museum. From the headquarters you can see a feeding station that opens to a small upland meadow bordered by witch hazel and laurel where 93 species have been identified. Besides the 14 birds of prey you might possibly see on a good day, a total of 241 species have been recorded since 1934, with over 70 species in residence during the breeding season. Anything that migrates over the eastern half of the United States is possible here—from Red-throated Loons to Lapland Longspurs.

Since record keeping began at Hawk Mountain in 1934, certain weather conditions have become associated with good hawk flights. These conditions should be checked before an outing is planned, for otherwise there might be a disappointed homeward-bound carload of visitors. A simple series of meteorological events usually guarantees a good day on the North Lookout. First, a low pressure system develops and passes north over New England, followed by a cold front that moves down from Canada. Finally, winds from the northwest blow for two or three days. Hawks have a good reason to fly on these days. Since the Appalachians and the Kittatinny Ridge generally run from northeast to southwest, the northwest winds strike the ridges at a nearly ninety-degree angle to produce uplifting air currents. The migrating hawks can fly hundreds of miles on these currents and expend little energy. So center your trip to Hawk Mountain around these days with northwest winds.

The harbingers of the fall season are the Bald Eagle and the Osprey. The Bald Eagles usually start passing the lookouts on their southbound trek by August 25, while the Ospreys are right behind them come early September. While stragglers are possible any time during the season, the Bald Eagle generally reaches its peak by September 25. The Osprey's peak days last a little longer, until the first week in October. In 1978, a representative year for both species, 33 Bald Eagles were sighted (5 in August and 20 in September), and 499 Ospreys passed Hawk Mountain (407 in September and 9 in August). Look high for both species. On the apparently warm and windless days of September, these two soar from ridge to ridge, sometimes reaching great heights on the thermals, which develop from the sun's heating of morning ground moisture. This heated moisture eventually rises to produce circulating air currents upon which soaring birds can ride.

The Broad-winged Hawk begins its migration by September and, year after year, reaches its apex in numbers between September 15 and 20. An all-time record was set a day early, on September 14, 1978, when 21,000 passed the lookouts. A total of 47,473 were tallied for the season, another new record, and their migration over Hawk Mountain was all but over by the second week of October. The Broad-wing is by far the most common migrant and can be seen riding the thermals in groups numbering into the hundreds. When this occurs, the Broad-wings are said to "kettle."

The other buteos don't come through as fast or as furiously, but they can be seen dependably at the right times. The Red-tailed Hawk, which averages about 4,000 a season, usually concentrates its migration between mid-October and mid-November, but can be seen any time during the season. The less common, but perhaps more handsome Red-shouldered Hawk comes past the lookouts from mid-October through the first week in November, numbering 300–500 per season. The largest and rarest of the buteos to fly by Hawk Mountain, the Rough-legged Hawk, has averaged between ten and fifteen a season since 1970. The best time to get a view of this rugged arctic visitor is from late October to mid-November.

The falcons of the east are not seen in great numbers at Hawk Mountain, because they prefer to migrate by the coastal route. The season totals for this family of birds at Cape May Point on the coast of New Jersey far surpass those at Hawk Mountain. The American Kestrel (Sparrow Hawk) passes the lookouts at the rate of 400–600 per season, and is seen from early September through mid-October. Both the Peregrine Falcon and Merlin (Pigeon Hawk) reflect the tendency toward coastal migration. Both average between 10 and 25 at Hawk Mountain, with an occasional swelling or dwindling in numbers. The Peregrine typically appears from September 25 through October 10, while the Merlin usually passes by about mid-October; but both are possible until mid-November.

The trend with the accipiters seems to be the same as the falcons. Much greater numbers of these can be seen at Cape May Point, with the exception of the Northern Goshawk. Nevertheless, the Sharp-shinned and Cooper's Hawks can be seen reliably at Hawk Mountain. The small, swift Sharpie numbers about 6,500 a year, with a record-breaking 12,804 sighted in 1977. They peak from late September through November 1, with stragglers any time during the season. The harder-to-identify Cooper's Hawk normally flies by at 250 per season, with its best time centering between late September and late October. Be careful in identifying the Cooper's, because its coloration is similar to the Sharp-shinned's, and the male Cooper's and female Sharpie are practically the same size. The adult Northern Goshawk, with its handsome coloration and fiery red eye, always creates a stir on the lookout. It averages about 60–100 a fall season, and is best seen from October 15 until November 15.

The Turkey Vulture can be identified throughout the season soaring high on the thermals in its characteristic dihedral wingspread. Present year-round, except for the coldest winter months, it is affectionately nicknamed the Kempton Eagle. The Northern Harrier's (Marsh Hawk's) migration period lasts throughout the fall season. Marshies usually number between 300 and 450 and are easily identified by their conspicuous white rumps.

King of birds, the Golden Eagle is a regular transient along the Appalachian Mountains come late fall. Although once more numerous, between 30 and 50 still fly by from mid-October until late November. This is the bird everyone hopes to see when they come to Hawk Mountain. Also keep an eye out for such rarities as the Swainson's Hawk and the arctic Gyrfalcon, which always surprise the visitors.

Hawks are the principal, but not the only, attraction during the fall season. Always be alert to the possibility of seeing other southbound migrants. Most herons, ducks, and geese of the northeast have been identified flying to the warmer climates. If you walk into a warbler wave in September, usually about 15 species are possible. These include Yellow-rumped (Myrtle), Magnolia, Blackpoll, Black-and-white, Blue-winged, Nashville, Black-throated Blue, Black-throated Green, Blackburnian, Chestnut-sided, Ovenbird, Northern Waterthrush, Kentucky, Canada, Redstart, and a few others. The creek and adjacent woods, just off Route 895 when turning right to Hawk Mountain, offer excellent habitat for warblers. Along the trail to the North Lookout, which is bordered by a blanket of rhododendron and mountain laurel, the resident Ruffed Grouse is possible in the early morning before the crowds arrive. The Hermit Thrush and Rufous-sided Towhee can often be detected sneaking through the underbrush. Common Nighthawks are frequently seen in the late afternoon, and Ruby-throated Hummingbirds buzz by with a quickness that begs, "Was that a Hummer?" On October 3, 1975, 48 Hummers were seen, with a total of 109 counted for the season. Hawk Mountain is probably the best spot in the region to catch passing Red-headed Wood-peckers: 63 were tallied for the 1977 season. Northern (Common) Ravens occasionally pass through, usually fewer than ten per year.

A variety of songbirds can best be seen at the headquarters feeding station from October on. Both White-breasted and (less commonly) Red-breasted Nuthatches alight on the feeders while Tufted Titmice and Black-capped Chickadees flit about. White-throated Sparrows and Dark-eyed (Slate-colored) Juncos rake the surrounding ground in search of food. Downy and sometimes Hairy Woodpeckers are seen clutching to the suet-filled logs, as Ruby-crowned and Golden-crowned Kinglets try to steal their way in for a taste. American Goldfinches and House and (occasionally) Purple Finches often compete at the feeders later in the season, while Cedar Waxwings gather late berries from the nearby bushes and trees. The secretive Brown Creeper can usually be found spiraling up trees, but you must look hard for it.

November is a good month to see the elusive crossbills and grosbeaks. Though never present in any great numbers, small flocks sometimes fly over and feed on the pine and hemlock cones around the lookouts. Both the Red and White-winged Crossbills have been known to stay around the lookouts for days. Pine Grosbeaks come through in smaller numbers, usually fewer than ten, and are sporadic all along the Kittatinny Ridge. Evening Grosbeaks fly in larger groups, but are also sporadic.

The end of November coincides with the end of the hawk flights, and Hawk Mountain goes into hibernation for the cold months ahead. Only the headquarters feeding station holds interest through the winter. December through February has hope for straggling flocks of Pine Siskins, Evening Grosbeaks, Common Redpolls, and Purple and House Finches, in addition to the other die-hard songbirds already mentioned.

The spring season starts in late April as warbler waves come through the woods and more than 70 other species begin to take up residence. This is with the notable exceptions of the Common Screech and Great Horned Owls, which are by this time finished with their breeding cycle. All the eastern warblers, with the understandable exceptions of the Kirtland's, Bachman's, and Swainson's, have been identified at Hawk Mountain, and 17 species call out territories for their nesting seasons. These include the Black-and-white, Worm-eating, Blue-winged, Nashville, Black-throated

Blue, Black-throated Green, Cerulean, Chestnut-sided, Ovenbird, Louisiana Waterthrush, Common Yellowthroat, Yellow-breasted Chat, Hooded, Canada, Redstart, occasionally the Golden-winged, and rarely the Brewster's. Check for the Golden-winged along the creek off Route 895 and in the lower foothills by the Schuylkill River.

All six vireos have been identified in migration, with only the common Red-eyed staying to nest. In addition, all eastern thrushes pass through, but just the American Robin and Wood Thrush breed. The woodpeckers are represented by five breeders—Common (Yellow-shafted) Flicker, Downy, the less common Hairy, Red-bellied, and Pileated. Look for the Pileated and listen for its distinctive call in the more remote parts of the refuge. While in those parts, also check for the Wild Turkey, another mountain woodlands nester. It is usually best to ask someone at headquarters, especially curator Alexander Nagy, which specific sites of breeders like the Pileated and Turkey to visit during a particular season. Yellow-billed and Black-billed Cuckoos nest here; they are common in areas that have been infested with caterpillars. American Wood-cock hide in the swampy and more moist wooded sections of the sanctuary.

When late May blooms in a fury of rhododendron, mountain laurel, and flowering dogwood, other common and colorful breed-ing birds come out. Northern (Baltimore) Oriole, Eastern Bluebird, Scarlet Tanager, Blue-gray Gnatcatcher, Indigo Bunting, Ameri-can Goldfinch, Ruby-throated Hummingbird, and the various war-blers create a visual extravaganza. Unless flushed, Whip-poor-wills are almost impossible to see during the day, but they can be heard at night. An interesting breeder is the Winter Wren; Hawk Mountain is perhaps one of its southernmost breeding grounds. Though not common, it is also present in the fall. Four flycatchers inhabit the sanctuary: Eastern Phoebe, Eastern (Wood) Pewee, and Great Crested and Least Flycatchers. Other Empidonax often come through on both migrations but move on to more suitable hab-itat. These are the Yellow-bellied, Willow, and Olive-sided Fly-catchers. The sparrows are thinly represented by only three nesters —Chipping, Field, and Song. All three can be seen around the headquarters area. Also look for breeding Cedar Waxwing in this berry-filled area. Although the Vesper Sparrow is very scarce as a breeder and not to be counted on, carefully check some of the lower meadows and pastures on both sides of Hawk Mountain for that bird.

In summary, the best time to see the most species of hawks during the fall is around mid-October. Stragglers of the earlier species like the Bald Eagle are then still filtering through, while many other species are peaking. If your main interest is concentrated hawk migration, mid-September is best for great numbers of Broadwings. Wear hiking boots for walking the rocky trail to the lookouts. High-powered binoculars and telescopes are useful for spotting longer-range birds. The day will also be more pleasant if you bring a lunch and something soft to sit on.

Bake Oven Knob

Bake Oven Knob sits atop the Kittatinny Ridge near New Tripoli, about fifteen miles northeast of Hawk Mountain. It offers an alternative to Hawk Mountain for those who wish to walk a shorter and more level trail to the lookouts. Bake Oven Knob's South Lookout is one-third of a mile from the parking area, and the North Lookout is only one-quarter of a mile further. All the species seen at Hawk Mountain are also possible here, and the crowds tend to be smaller than at the more famous spot. The same weather conditions apply here as at Hawk Mountain, so look for cold fronts followed by northwesterly breezes when planning an outing.

For additional information, and Hawk Mountain's birdlist, write:

Hawk Mountain Sanctuary
Route 2
Kempton, Pa. 19529
Phone: (215) 756-3431

Directions to Hawk Mountain and Bake Oven Knob

From the City Line Avenue entrance onto Interstate 76 West (Schuylkill Expressway), drive west to the Valley Forge–King of Prussia entrance to the Pennsylvania Turnpike. After the toll booth bear left for I-76 West to Harrisburg. Drive 28.6 miles to the Morgantown Exit (Exit 22). Bear right and loop around the ramp for 0.4 miles to the toll booth (80¢ in 1979).

Make a left at the stop sign on Route 10 just past the toll. Drive 0.3 miles to the next stop sign and make a right onto Route 23 West. Travel 0.4 miles through Morgantown and turn right onto Interstate 176 for Reading. Continue 11 miles along I-176, and then bear left at Route 422 West for Reading (Exit 4 West). Proceed through Reading on Route 422 West for 4.9 miles and then bear left for Route 222 North for Allentown and Pottsville. Avoid turning right for Route 422 West to Lebanon! Drive 2.1 miles on Route 222 North, make a right onto Route 61 North for Pottsville, and drive 19.1 miles along Route 61 North (through Hamburg) to Route 895. Turn right onto Route 895 East for Drehersville and drive another 2.5 miles to the sign for Hawk Mountain Sanctuary. Make a right, cross the bridge, and travel 0.3 miles to a crossroads. Bear left here and continue up the steep grade for 1.6 miles to the headquarters. A one-way trip from Philadelphia to Hawk Mountain takes approximately two hours.

To reach Bake Oven Knob, take Route 309 North out of Philadelphia to Allentown, Pennsylvania. Stay on Route 309 North past Allentown and proceed to Route 143. Drive 2 miles on Route 309 North past this intersection and turn right onto County Road 39056. Travel 2.1 miles along this road and then turn left onto an unmarked road by some houses and out-buildings. Continue up the steep grade (dirt road in parts) to the Bake Oven Knob parking lot.

Map 7
Hawk Mountain Sanctuary

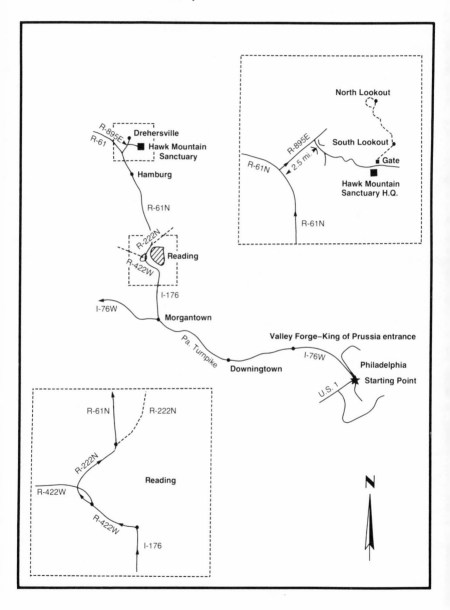

Map 8
View Looking East from the North Lookout, Hawk Mountain Sanctuary

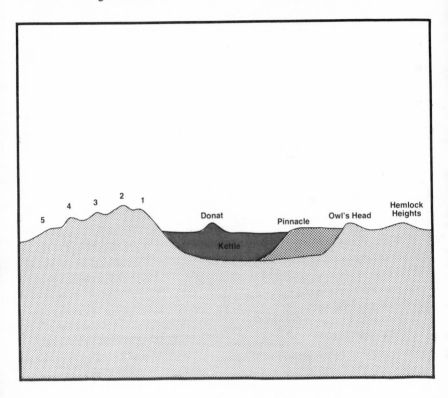

Brigantine
National Wildlife Refuge
and Brigantine Island,
New Jersey

Brigantine National Wildlife Refuge

Brigantine National Wildlife Refuge, located in Atlantic County, New Jersey, was established in 1939 for the protection and management of waterfowl along the Atlantic flyway. It was originally created to aid the Brant and American Black Duck, which have since increased. Brant have rebounded from their critical lows in the 1930s caused by blight to their winter staple of eelgrass. Many species use the refuge year-round; the waterfowl population surpasses 150,000 birds during the winter.

This 20,229-acre preserve consists primarily of coastal salt marshes interwoven with tidal bays and channels. Approximately 1,600 acres of marsh have been diked into two large fresh-water pools fed by upland runoff and precipitation. These impoundments attract great concentrations of waterfowl and marshbirds, which can be observed from the surrounding dike tour route. Several hundred acres of upland habitat form the western border of the refuge, providing cover and nesting sights for various landbirds.

Brigantine's diverse habitats of fresh- and salt-water marshes, impoundments, open bays, upland brush, and woodlands account for the 270 bird species identified on the refuge. An additional forty species—including windblown pelagics, western strays, and European waifs—have been seen at the refuge. Brigantine serves as a coastal magnet for rarities, providing local birders with the excitement of unexpected "lifers."

The spring and fall migrations are best for seeing the greatest number as well as variety of birds. Big Day counts at Brigantine during the second week in May should exceed one hundred species, including waterfowl, shorebirds, and upland species. Nowhere else in the Delaware Valley region, except perhaps Bombay Hook or Cape May, is the birdwatcher likely to see as many water- and landbirds together. Every season provides unique birding opportunities. Many spring migrants remain to breed during the summer months—over one hundred species have nested on the refuge or in the immediate area (nesters are designated † after the species). Using the refuge as its focus, the 1977 Christmas Count totaled 133 species.

Much of Brigantine consists of salt marshes and channels that are relatively inaccessible—unless you are a duck hunter or a fisherman. However, an eight-mile auto tour samples all the preserve's habitats and affords a view of their representative birdlife. Immediately after entering the tour route by the headquarters, walk the Leeds Eco-trail off to the right (see the pamphlet available at the visitors' center). Fifty yards further along the road take a side trip to Gull Pond and the West Tower. This flooded gravel pit is heavily used by gulls and ducks and the observation tower allows a panoramic survey of the refuge.

The one-way auto tour around the dikes then proceeds along the southern edge of the 900-acre West Pool for one mile. Seasonal regulation of the pool's water level controls plant growth and thus its attraction to waterfowl. During the cooler months, the freshwater West Pool seems more like an open lake, hosting rafts of migrating and wintering waterfowl. With water levels down, especially during late summer, the exposed mudflats seduce large numbers of shorebirds.

The South Tower marks the halfway point along the South Dike. Here a crossdike separates the East and West Pools and is reserved for wildlife photography—ask about blind permits at the headquarters. To the right of the dikes are expansive salt marshes crisscrossed by a myriad of tidal channels. Opposite the South Tower, Turtle Cove (an extension of Reed's Bay) interrupts these cordgrass meadows almost bathing the dike itself. Horseshoe Crabs litter this sandy beach in early June and the sheltered cove beyond attracts wintering seafowl during the colder months.

The South Dike continues another mile or so with the East Pool to its left. The 700-acre East Pool serves as a major waterfowl breeding area. This pool, with its low nesting islands and freshwater potholes, seems more land than water, and its extensive mudflats swarm with migrating shorebirds.

The route now turns sharply to the left for three-quarters of a mile as the East Dike. Some 200 yards east of this corner is a birding hot spot called "Godwit Corner." Shallow pools dot the salt meadows here, with Marbled and Hudsonian Godwits and the American Avocet appearing during their late summer movement.

Perch Cove, an extension of Little Bay, forces the dike road again to the left; you are now on the North Dike. This salt-water bay flanks the dike for one-half mile and is good for wintering sea ducks and Brant. The North Dike borders the East Pool to its left for a mile until the intersection with the crossdike. Here an informal parking lot allows the birder to scope the vast West Pool before him. After a short curve, the North Dike straightens for its last mile-and-a-quarter leg along the West Pool.

The character of the tour route changes dramatically at the end of the West Pool. During the colder months, Golden and Bald Eagles frequently roost among the stunted trees overlooking the large excavation pool at Station 11. The sentinel line of trees separating this pool from the adjoining marshes hosts a yearly blitz of spring warblers. To the left, a peregrine hacking sight has replaced the former osprey nesting pole. Birds raised in captivity have been released here for the past several years in an effort to reestablish the Peregrine Falcon in the area.

Up a short incline, to the right of the road, extensive upland brush takes over. Approximately one-quarter of a mile further, a small fresh-water creek courses under the road. Park here and walk the foot trail off to the left. This green-belted slough attracts swarms of migrant landbirds. The Experimental Pool, with edgings of cattails, reeds, and other marsh vegetation, greets the birder shortly. Landbirds to the left, marshbirds to the right!

Bordered by brush and sloping meadows, the road continues another half-mile or so to a large stand of woods, which envelops the winding road for the next half-mile. Pine and oak predominate, forming a canopy over the thick, dark understory. Several walking trails that lead off from the main route afford glimpses of the region's landbirds.

Immediately after leaving the woods, the road crosses Doughty Creek—a major source of fresh water for the impoundments. Wildlife trails radiate from the small (two-car) parking lot twenty yards past the bridge. One excellent foot trail borders the marshes along Doughty Creek, which is more of a pond at this point. Various fresh-water marshbirds can be seen here—if you are patient. The walk meanders past several tiny wading pools, including the back-side of Gull Pond. Isolated patches of trees and brush provide nesting sites for landbirds that require more openness than the dark woods afford.

Another nearby trail, known as the Foot Path, angles off at the tour road's end. Mixed stands of conifers and hardwoods cover the slopes to the right of the trail. Dense tangles and intermediate-height trees separate the path from a wild cranberry bog to the left. A walk here during the second week in May promises hordes of spring migrants, especially warblers.

The tour is now completed. To leave the refuge, turn right onto Great Creek Road, or make a left for the short loop back to the headquarters.

Birding is excellent year-round, especially during the spring and fall migrations. Heavy coverage by birders provides extensive knowledge of the refuge's wildlife. The Delaware Valley Birding Hot Line, at (215) 567-BIRD, highlights each week's more interesting observations. Check the visitors' center near headquarters, where a grid map and daily sighting list provide up-to-the-minute information.

A scope is essential for scanning the pools, bays, and mudflats. This can be done right from the dikes and observation towers. A windbreaker in the winter and insect repellent in the summer minimize seasonal drawbacks to comfortable birdwatching. You should spend the entire day at the refuge, although the tour itself can be completed in two hours.

The first warm days in mid-March herald the arrival of spring. Waterfowl, staging their northern migration, greatly increase—especially on the West Pool. Good concentrations of Pied-billed Grebe,† Canada† and Snow Geese, Mallard,† American Black Duck,† Gadwall,† Common Pintail,† Green-winged† and Blue-winged† Teals, American Wigeon, Northern Shoveler,† Greater Scaup, Bufflehead, Ruddy Duck,† and American Coot† frequent the impoundments. Lesser numbers of Mute† and (occasionally) Whistling Swans, Wood Duck,† and Hooded and Common Mergansers are also present in these fresh-water pools. Redhead, Ring-necked Duck, Canvasback, and Lesser Scaup are sometimes seen. The adjacent salt-water bays, Perch and Turtle Coves, host large numbers of Horned Grebe, Brant, Greater Scaup, Common Goldeneye, Bufflehead, and Red-breasted Merganser. White-winged, Surf, and Black (Common) Scoters, Oldsquaw, and Common and Red-throated Loons are more reliably seen in the Atlantic surf off the jetties at nearby Brigantine Island.

Mid-April marks the wading-bird invasion. Great Blue† and Little Blue† Herons, Cattle Egret, Great† (Common) and Snowy† Egrets, Louisiana† and Black-crowned Night† Herons, and Glossy Ibis† are commonly seen along the dikes or roosting in the East Pool shrubbery. The Green Heron† favors the Doughty Creek area, while the Yellow-crowned Night Heron† is seen only a few times a season. Least† and American† Bitterns frequent extensive stands of reeds—especially those bordering the Experimental Pool. But they are very secretive and rarely observed.

Mid-April also signals the beginning of the shorebird migration. Although most species peak during early May, American Oystercatcher,† American Woodcock,† Common Snipe,† and Whimbrel seem more common now. American Woodcock† and Common Snipe† favor the wet upland habitat around Doughty Creek, while the American Oystercatcher† and Whimbrel are equally at home on the East Pool mudflats or the nearby salt meadows.

The first two weeks in May are unbelievable. Every available beach and mudflat is crowded with migrating shorebirds—especially the East Pool and the drier edges of the West Pool. Semipalmated Plover, Killdeer,† Black-bellied Plover, Spotted Sandpiper,† Willet,† Greater and Lesser Yellowlegs, Dunlin, Short-billed Dowitcher, Least and Semipalmated Sandpipers, and Sanderling are certain to be seen. Solitary Sandpiper, Red Knot, Pectoral Sandpiper, and White-rumped Sandpiper (late May through early June) occur, but more sporadically. Hordes of Ruddy Turnstones work the beach along Turtle Cove from late May through early June, while individual Ruff and Northern and Wilson's Phalaropes unpredictably visit the impoundments from May through September. The Curlew Sandpiper appears in singles every year, usually during the last ten days in May. Other species not mentioned above may occur during their fall migration.

The elusive King and Virginia† Rails and Sora† are present in the fresh and brackish marshes along Doughty Creek and the Experimental Pool during May, although it takes luck to actually see them. Common Gallinule† and Clapper Rail† present no such problem. The Common Gallinule† religiously forages along the impoundments' marshy edges, while the Clapper Rail† darts out from the salt meadows during low tide.

While traveling the dikes, keep an eye out for birds overhead. The Osprey† circles high over the bays, while the Northern Harrier† (Marsh Hawk) quarters the marshes below. Greater Black-backed, Herring,† Ring-billed, and Laughing† Gulls are usually seen. Common,† Forster's,† and Little† (Least) Terns and Black Skimmer† are to be expected, while the Gull-billed Tern† is being increasingly reported every year. The Black Tern is infrequently seen during the spring migration, but is a regular late summer visitor.

The landbird contingent is also well represented during early to mid-May. Large numbers of thrushes, vireos, and warblers pass through the refuge's upland habitats during spring migration. Several foot trails can be rewarding hot spots for migrants, including those around the excavation pool at Station 11 and the walk to the Experimental Pool. At the tour's end, the Doughty Creek trail and the Foot Path along the bog are a must. All the trails are safe, convenient, and easily walked in one-half hour.

All eastern thrushes can be seen, although less reliably than at such inland locales as Ridley Creek State Park and Princeton. Of the Vireos, only the White-eyed,† Solitary (in late April), and Red-eyed† are to be expected. Black-and-white,† Blue-winged,† Northern Parula, Yellow,† Magnolia, Black-throated Blue, Yellow-rumped (Myrtle), Blackpoll, Pine,† Prairie,† and Palm (April) Warblers, Ovenbird,† Northern Waterthrush, Common Yellowthroat,† American Redstart, and Canada Warbler are common. Tennessee, Nashville, Cape May, Black-throated Green, Blackburnian, Chestnut-sided, Bay-breasted, Yellow-breasted Chat,† Hooded,† and Wilson's Warblers are less frequently seen. Common Bobwhite,† Ruby-throated Hummingbird, Belted Kingfisher,† Fish† and American† (Common) Crows, Blue-gray Gnatcatcher, Golden-crowned and Ruby-crowned Kinglets (late April), Cedar Waxwing, Northern (Baltimore) Oriole, Scarlet Tanager,† Rose-breasted Grosbeak, lingering Dark-eyed Junco, and American Tree and White-throated Sparrows round out a successful May day.

May is a transition month for birding. In addition to the spring migrants passing through, many summering birds begin nesting now. Various breeding members of the woodpecker, flycatcher, swallow, wren, blackbird, finch, and sparrow families are likely to be seen on a spring trip and will be discussed shortly.

Summer begins in mid-June and is officially welcomed by biting greenflies along the dikes and mosquitoes patrolling the upland trails. Birding is most comfortable on cool, breezy days, which tend to scatter the insects.

Both impoundments, the tidal channels, and Doughty Creek are crowded with broods of ducks and geese. Many of the ducks seen during the spring migration remain in smaller numbers to breed. But several species have virtually disappeared as summer residents over the past five years, including Pied-billed Grebe, Green-winged Teal, Northern Shoveler, and Ruddy Duck. Check the nesting boxes along Doughty Creek for Wood Duck.† Egrets and herons are everywhere, while various bitterns and rails nest in the dense marsh vegetation. The Willet† is the noisiest and most common of the summering shorebirds, while Forster's,† Common,† and Little† Terns and Black Skimmer† are frequently seen along the dikes. Check the northwest corner of the West Pool for the Gull-billed Tern.† Several pairs have nested in this area for the past few years.

The upland habitat along the refuge's western border hosts many nesting landbirds. Downy Woodpecker,† Blue Jay,† Carolina Chickadee,† Tufted Titmouse,† Carolina Wren,† Wood Thrush,† Red-eyed Vireo,† Black-and-white† and Pine† Warblers, Oven-bird,† and Rufous-sided Towhee† are common summer residents of the dense pine-oak forest along the tour route. Yellow-billed† and Black-billed† Cuckoos, Great Crested Flycatcher,† Eastern (Wood) Pewee,† White-breasted Nuthatch,† Hooded Warbler,† and Scarlet Tanager† are occasionally seen. Common (Yellow-shafted) Flicker,† Eastern Kingbird,† House Wren,† Northern Mockingbird,† Gray Catbird,† Brown Thrasher,† American Robin,† White-eyed Vireo,† Yellow† and Prairie† Warblers, Common Yellowthroat,† Yellow-breasted Chat,† Common Grackle,† Northern Cardinal,† Indigo Bunting,† American Goldfinch,† and Chipping,† Field,† and Song† Sparrows favor the more open second-growth areas and brushy hedgerows along Doughty Creek, Station 11, and the Foot Path. The trail leading to the Experimental Pool is especially good for White-eyed Vireo,† Yellow Warbler,† Common Yellowthroat,† American Goldfinch,† and Swamp Sparrow,† which frequent the tangles bordering the small creek.

Tree† and Barn† Swallows abound, hawking insects over the fields and marshes. Every year, Purple Martins† colonize the martin house by the headquarters.

The Marsh (Long-billed Marsh) Wren† sings from the reed and cattail patches, especially those along the Experimental Pool and the northern border of the East Pool. Eastern Meadowlark,† Red-winged Blackbird,† and Sharp-tailed† and Seaside† Sparrows are common breeders in the salt and brackish marshes along the dikes. "Psshing" and combing the cordgrass meadows are often necessary to flush these last two secretive birds.

August signals the beginning of the fall migration. The impoundments, now extensive mudflats, are covered with shorebirds from late July until well into October. The spring transients are more plentiful now, while other species visit only during their autumnal movement. Pectoral, Western, and Stilt Sandpipers (the last as early as mid-July) are common August migrants, and the Lesser (American) Golden Plover is an occasional Labor Day visitor. Upland Sandpiper (Plover) and Buff-breasted and Baird's Sandpipers are recorded most years—usually as singles. August is also a good time for Wilson's and Northern Phalaropes and an occasional Ruff along the mudflats. Marbled and Hudsonian Godwits and American Avocet are regularly seen at "Godwit Corner"; the American Avocet prefers late September. Around October 1 the Short-billed Dowitcher movement tapers off, while the Long-billed Dowitcher increases as fall progresses.

The shorebird migration continues into early September, coinciding with the major landbird flight southward. In addition to the returning spring migrants mentioned before, the birder may glimpse Connecticut and Wilson's Warblers, which occur more frequently (although still not commonly) during September. Check the refuge's marshes for Bobolink, Rusty Blackbird (mid-October), and Savannah Sparrow. Practically every year a few Yellow-headed Blackbirds are seen at Brigantine during the late summer or early fall.

Tern concentrations dramatically increase in August and September. Black Terns are common now, while sporadic Royal and Caspian Terns add to the excitement.

The last weekend in September marks the peak of the southbound falcon migration. American Kestrel† (Sparrow Hawk), Merlin (Pigeon Hawk), and an occasional wild Peregrine Falcon are to be expected along the dikes and upland trails. Sharp-shinned and, rarely, Cooper's Hawks, buteos, Northern Harrier,† and Osprey† are common migrants.

The southward flow of ducks, Canada Geese,† and Brant picks up during October. The impoundments and tidal channels attract large congregations of migrating waterfowl, while shorebirds and waders rapidly decline.

Winter sneaks into Brigantine during November. Snow Geese, including occasional members of the Blue race, now complement the awaiting Canada Geese† and Brant. Spectacular flights of these large white birds whirl across the dark November sky like flashing venetian blinds. Most duck species are more abundant now than in spring—some of the hardier individuals stay the winter. Horned Grebe, Brant, Greater and Lesser Scaup, Common Goldeneye, Bufflehead, and Red-breasted Merganser frequent the salt-water bays from November through March. Pied-billed Grebe,† Canada† and Snow Geese, Mallard,† American Black Duck,† Gadwall,† Common Pintail,† Green-winged† and Blue-winged† Teals, American Wigeon, Northern Shoveler,† Ruddy Duck,† and American Coot,† and Common and Hooded Mergansers are commonly seen now on ice-free sections of the impoundments. Other birds seen include Whistling Swan, Ring-necked Duck, Canvasback and, rarely, the Redhead. Single Common (European) Teal, now considered a race of the Green-winged, and Eurasian (European) Wigeon occur annually during late fall and winter.

Great Blue Heron,† Dunlin, and Sanderling are the only shorebirds that can be reliably expected during the coldest months. Straggling Great Egret,† Black-crowned Night Heron,† American Bittern,† Clapper† and Virginia† Rails, Killdeer,† Black-bellied Plover, Common Snipe,† Greater and Lesser Yellowlegs, and various sandpipers are sometimes encountered.

The Northern Harrier† is the most common bird of prey during the winter. Several are always seen along the dikes, while individual Rough-legged Hawks and Short-eared Owls are frequently observed patrolling the marshes. American Kestrel† and Red-tailed Hawk round out the winter raptor contingent. Most years, Bald and Golden Eagles visit the refuge in very small numbers from December through February. When not scanning the refuge from perches at Station 11, these magnificent birds quarter the marshes and pools from great heights. During its cyclic southern excur-

sions, the Snowy Owl is occasionally seen surveying the meadows
from a grassy knoll.

The mixed conifer-hardwood forest along the upland tour route
is generally quiet during the winter. The silence is broken by gypsy
bands of Downy Woodpecker,† Carolina Chickadee,† Tufted
Titmouse,† Golden-crowned and Ruby-crowned Kinglets, White-
breasted† and Red-breasted Nuthatches, and the secretive Brown
Creeper. Evening Grosbeak, Pine Siskin and, rarely, Red and
White-winged Crossbills are sometimes seen working the pines
during invasion years. The thickets below the canopy are frequented by American Robin,† Northern Cardinal,† Fox and White-
throated Sparrows, plus an occasional Hermit Thrush and Carolina Wren.† The more open brushy hedgerows along the various
foot trails provide food and shelter for Northern Mockingbird,†
Myrtle Warbler, American Goldfinch,† Dark-eyed (Slate-colored)
Junco, and American Tree, Field,† White-throated, and Song†
Sparrows. Open fields and marshes host wintering Horned Lark,†
Eastern Meadowlark,† Savannah and Swamp† Sparrows, and an
occasional flock of Snow Buntings. The well-supplied feeder by
the headquarters is a good spot to observe Purple Finch and the
more common House Finch.

Brigantine Island

Brigantine Island, approximately ten miles from the National Wildlife Refuge, is an excellent birding locale, especially during the
winter. A long boulder jetty reaches out into the Atlantic surf from
the island's southern tip. Extensive sand dunes planted with coastal
grasses border the jetty entrance, but they are rapidly dwindling
due to summer home construction.

**Heading towards the refuge on Route 9 North from Delilah
Road, make a right onto Route 30 East towards Atlantic City.
Travel 5.8 miles on Route 30 East (White Horse Pike), bearing
right at the sign for Brigantine Island. Quickly (0.1 mile later)
make a left at the first light, looping across Route 30. Travel
another 0.6 miles and make a left at the stop sign. Drive 2.2
miles to Harbor Beach Blvd.—crossing the four-lane bridge to
the island along the way. Make a right onto Harbor Beach**

Blvd. and travel 1.7 miles to the parking lot near the jetty. This lot may soon become a private drive because of home building. In that case, cut off Harbor Beach Blvd. toward the ocean and walk south along the beach toward the jetty.

The sandy beaches and dunes near the jetty are prime habitat for breeding Piping Plover.† During the winter, the grassier portions host Savannah and Ipswich Sparrows and Horned Lark.† Flocks of Snow Bunting, with an occasional Lapland Longspur, also frequent this area.

Greater Black-backed, Herring,† and Ring-billed Gulls are seen throughout the year, with an occasional Glaucous or Iceland Gull appearing during the winter. Bonaparte's Gull is a frequent winter visitor off the jetty, while the Laughing Gull† is present only during the warmer months. For the past few years, a summering Black-headed Gull has been seen near the southern tip of the island.

Flocks of Purple Sandpiper work the surf-bathed jetty from November through early May. The Oldsquaw abounds during the colder months, while Common and Red-throated Loons are sometimes seen in the ocean. On the calmer bay side of the jetty, wintering Brant, Greater and Lesser Scaup, Common Goldeneye, Bufflehead, and Red-breasted Merganser are to be expected. Rarely, Common and King Eiders ride the breakers nearby. Small flights of all three Scoters pass the jetty tip like clockwork October through April, but a scope is necessary for positive identification. Look for the Double-crested Cormorant here during its spring and fall movements.

Check the bay inlets and mudflats under the main bridge for American Oystercatcher† and Royal Tern, which often gather here in large numbers from mid-August through September.

Leeds Point Road

For the past several years, breeding Chuck-will's-widows† have been heard calling along Leeds Point Road next to the refuge. Listen for this bird's distinctive call between dusk and dawn from June through mid-July. This area is also one of the most reliable spots in the region to hear (see?) the Whip-poor-will,† which is common in the open scrubby woodlands bordering the refuge.

Leeds Point Road is the first right (0.1 miles) past the Great Creek Road entrance to the refuge along Route 9 North. Both birds can also be heard along other nearby roads, including Great Creek Road (immediately before the refuge gate) and Lily Lake Road.

For more information, and the refuge birdlist, write:

Brigantine National Wildlife
   Refuge
Great Creek Road, P.O. Box 72
Oceanville, N.J. 08231
Phone: (609) 652-1665

Directions to Brigantine National Wildlife Refuge

Only eleven miles from Atlantic City, Brigantine N.W.R. is within a sixty mile, one and one-half hour drive of Philadelphia. From the City Line Avenue entrance onto Interstate 76 East (Schuylkill Expressway), travel 10.4 miles, following the signs for New Jersey to the toll booth at the Walt Whitman Bridge. After paying the toll (60¢ in 1979), cross the bridge and drive 2.1 miles to the sign for the North-South Freeway and Atlantic City. Bear left at this sign and continue 2.4 miles to Route 42 South for Atlantic City. Drive 7.8 miles along Route 42 South and bear left onto the Atlantic City Expressway. Travel 26.6 miles to the Great Egg Harbor toll booth ($1.00 in 1979) and continue another 7.6 miles to Exit 9 for Absecon. Drive 0.2 miles along the exit ramp and make a left onto Delilah Road at the stop sign. Go 0.55 miles along Delilah Road to the first traffic circle, drive halfway around (0.1 miles), and continue straight ahead following the signs for Brigantine. Travel 3.5 miles to the second light at Route 9 North (New Road). Make a left onto New Road and continue 1.6 miles to the intersection with Route 30. Pass through the intersection at Route 30 and drive 1 mile to North Shore Road through the town of Absecon. Route 9 North is also called New Road and E. Wyoming Avenue as it courses through town. Bear left onto North Shore Road, which is actually a continuation of Route 9 North. Follow the signs for Manahawkin and travel 3 miles on Route 9 North to the Oceanville Post Office. At the Post Office make a right onto Great Creek Road and go another 1.4 miles to the refuge headquarters.

An alternative route is to take the Vine Street Exit off Interstate 76 East (Schuylkill Expressway). Follow the signs and cross the Ben Franklin Bridge (toll 60¢ in 1979). Take Route 30 East (White Horse Pike) to Route 9 North in the town of Absecon. Make a left onto Route 9 North and proceed as before. This way saves $2.00 in tolls (round trip), but takes longer and lacks the rural scenery of the Atlantic City Expressway.

Map 9
Directions to Brigantine National Wildlife Refuge

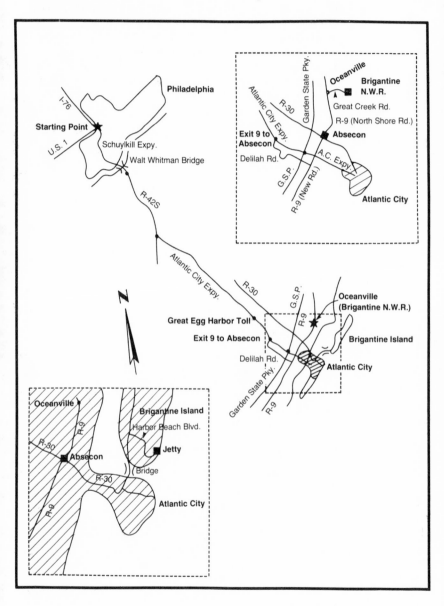

Map 10
Brigantine National Wildlife Refuge

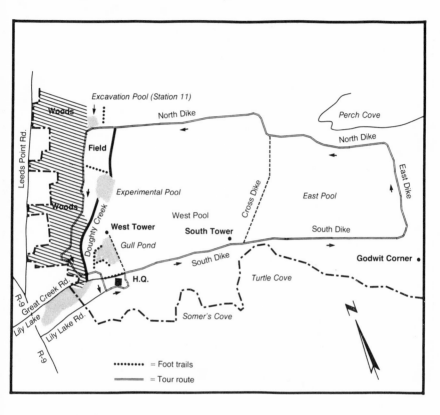

Cape May Point State Park and Higbee Beach, New Jersey

Cape May Point State Park

Cape May Point, New Jersey, presents to the visiting birder a fall migration extravaganza that is matched by few other places in North America. Strategically located along the Atlantic flyway, Cape May Point State Park sits on the southernmost edge of the Cape May Peninsula. The park was originally used as a lighthouse station beginning in 1823. During World War II a military defense base and radio installation for the Atlantic Fleet was located here. The land was turned over to New Jersey in 1963 and converted into a state park. It now includes 300 acres where hiking, fishing, picnicking, and birding are all permitted. A series of short, color-marked trails, up to two miles long, snakes through the brackish marsh and accompanying wooded areas to provide access to the more remote sections of the park. A new, modern nature center near the lighthouse explains the delicate natural history of the region.

Between Cape May and the Delaware coast lie eighteen miles of Delaware Bay. For the southbound fall migrants, this means a long nonstop flight without food and the threat of being blown out to sea. Thus, Cape May is the perfect staging area for the birds to rest and fuel up. Of more importance, especially to the birder, the migrants wait for the ideal wind and weather conditions to cross the bay. On these days, birds gather by the thousands and literally cover the point.

The diversity of ecosystems around the park can support not only a great concentration of birds but also a great variety of species. Fresh-water ponds for ducks and geese, brackish marshes for herons, egrets, rails, and bitterns, swamps for lowland birds, open fields, deciduous thickets, and pine woodlots for songbirds, beaches and mudflats for shorebirds, and open ocean for gulls, terns, and sea ducks are all available. At least 363 species have been identified over the years, and a good day during the fall migration should produce about 100 species. Every season offers opportunities at Cape May, but fall and winter are by far the best. Even the seemingly dead winter months are alive with birds. The Christmas Bird Count, conducted by the Delaware Valley Ornithological Club, has recently (1972–1979) averaged 140 species, and has identified as many as 155. The area's representative spring migrants and summer breeders can be reliably seen closer to Philadelphia at such places as Brigantine National Wildlife Refuge.

Over the years, unofficial and spotty hawk counts were kept at Cape May. Since the coastline is a major raptor migration route, in September 1976 the New Jersey Audubon Society initiated official daily counts for the fall hawk flights. In only four years' time it has become clear that Cape May is the raptor capital of North America, surpassing even Hawk Mountain in numbers of birds.

Hawk flights at Cape May seem to follow the same weather trend as at Hawk Mountain. That is, cold fronts pass over New England, followed by northwest winds. Good flights can be expected on these days with northwest winds. The best vantage points to see hawks from are the areas in front of the lighthouse and the dunes in back of Higbee Beach, a couple of miles up the coast on the Delaware Bay side. The hawk migration gets under way as early as late August, when Ospreys start to filter through. Averaging 1,000 a season since 1976, they are most reliably seen from September through mid-October.

The eastern falcons prefer the coastal route for migration, and a numbers comparison with other hawk lookouts bears this out. The American Kestrel (Sparrow Hawk) passes the Cape from early September until early November, averaging about 12,000. This is compared to an average of 400–600 per season at Hawk Mountain. The same trend is seen with the Merlin (Pigeon Hawk). Its peak period begins in late September, continues through October, and has averaged 750 since 1976. But at Hawk Mountain, 25 is considered normal for this species! The Peregrine Falcon has been showing up at Cape May in greater numbers than at any other hawk watch. A record 230, including many immatures, migrated through in 1979, with the great majority seen between late September and late October. Cape May is the best place to see your Peregrine.

The buteos seem to prefer the inland route, but Cape May still produces good numbers of all species. The Red-tailed Hawk numbers about 1,600 a season, peaking between mid-October and mid-November, although it is possible all season. The smaller Broadwings can be seen "kettling" in great numbers beginning around September 20 until early October. Numbers fluctuate from year to year. In 1976, a total of 1,462 were recorded, while in 1977 the number swelled to 12,402. Red-shouldered Hawks can be seen from mid-October to mid-November. They average about 400 a season, while the 1976 season produced an unexpected 700. Rough-legged Hawks are rare—usually less than ten are seen each season, typically in late October through mid-November, although a few stay for the cold winter months. A western visitor seems to be turning up year after year, at least since 1973. The handsome Swainson's Hawk delights and surprises birders by making appearances, usually singly, in October and November. Keep your eyes out for this one.

Two accipiter species pass Cape May in impressive numbers, surpassing every other hawk watch in numbers. Sharp-shinned Hawks are by far the most common raptor here, with an astounding 32,610 recorded in 1978 and a mind-boggling 48,447 flying through in 1979, 4,608 identified on October 14 alone. Look for the Sharpies to peak between late September and early November. The Cooper's Hawk tells another staggering story. During the first four years of official counts, and for some years earlier, the seasonal count here exceeded the combined totals of all other hawk watches in the northeastern United States, even doubling the combined totals. In 1977, 864 were identified, in 1978, 668, and, in 1979, 1,875 at Cape May. Cape May is clearly the Cooper's Hawk capital of North America. The best time to see this accipiter is between late September and late October. The largest of the group, the Northern Goshawk, prefers the inland migration route via the Kittatinny Ridge. Averaging about twenty a season at Cape May, the best time to see a Northern Goshawk is from mid-October to mid-November.

Both the Golden and Bald Eagles come by the point in small numbers; fewer than twenty individuals per season can be expected. The Golden Eagle's peak is from mid-October to mid-November, but individuals are possible throughout the winter. Bald Eagles peak from mid-September until November 1, with stragglers possible through November. Northern Harriers (Marsh Hawks) are equally distributed throughout the three count months (1,425 in 1979, 761 in 1978), and Turkey Vultures are possible any time during the fall.

One aspect of Cape May that adds to its scientific interest is the nighttime capture and banding of owls. While most birders will not be on hand for this, the numbers provide a good insight to the birds present that, unless spooked, are not usually seen during the day. Owl banding takes place in October and November, in addition to hawk banding throughout the season. Barn, Long-eared, and Saw-whet Owls are most commonly caught. Barn Owls have averaged between 50 and 60 banded, while Long-ears and Saw-whets number 30–50 a season. There are fluctuations in numbers from year to year, and of course more birds get by the traps than are caught.

Taking a break from hawk watching, there are still more great birding possibilities at the state park. Walking the gravel road in front of the visitors' center, continue to the giant sand dunes that stretch for several hundred yards separating the beach front from the tidal marshes. A tripod and high-powered scope are very useful here. Set up by the concrete defense fortress and scan the tidal marsh and pond in front. From mid-September on through the fall migration, many species rest and feed on this pond. Great Blue, Green, Black-crowned Night, Little Blue, and sometimes Louisiana Herons can all be seen from this vantage point. In addition, Snowy, Great (Common), and Cattle Egrets are always fishing the area. American Coot, Mute Swan, Mallard, American Black Duck, Gadwall, Common Pintail, Green-winged Teal, American Wigeon, and Northern Shoveler are usually paddling around. Blue-winged Teal can be found, but in much lesser numbers. Glossy Ibis and Canada Geese search for food near the water's edge, and the less common but always reliable Pied-billed Grebe dives in the deeper waters. American and Least Bitterns are hiding in the marshes in good numbers. Walking the periphery of the pond through the tall reed forest during September will almost guarantee that you spook these two species. Cape May is one of the best places in the region for the Least Bittern. It would be a good idea to wear high rubber boots while doing this because the hike will be a muddy one. Clapper Rails and less often King Rails skitter through the reeds at the marshes' edge, but it takes a good eye to catch them.

Turn your scope toward the ocean and other species are possible. All three scoters—Black (Common), White-winged, and Surf—are floating on the surf from mid- to late September on through the winter months. At this time, the gulls are represented by wintering Herring, Ring-billed, and Greater Black-backed. Bonaparte's Gulls are occasionally seen flying by, usually in small flocks, characterized by their erratic tern-like flight and triangular white wingtips. Terns have all but gone by October. Earlier in the fall season, about September 1, look for Common, Little (Least), Forster's, and small groups of Royal Terns. Cape May is one of the better places in the region for the latter species. Black Terns have come through by late August with a few stragglers possible later. Double-crested Cormorants fly by at steady intervals but take patience to see.

Shorebirds flock at Cape May, finding adequate feeding grounds on the beach front and mudflats, and in the shallow waters of the ponds. Many species are possible, but specific times during the fall migration are best for a few. Late August and very early September are optimal times for the Buff-breasted Sandpiper. Not found every year, this is one of the rarer migrants at Cape May. This shorebird favors the Mercer Sod Farm (see Other Birding Hot Spots), with Lesser (American) Golden Plover and Upland Sandpiper (Plover) as traveling companions. Grassy fields and meadows, especially those on the road to Higbee Beach and surrounding the state park, are best for all three species. Also look for them in the cow pasture that borders the eastern edge of the park, several hundred yards up the sand dunes from the defense base. A total of eight Buff-breasted Sandpipers were identified on September 2, 1977, at the point. Lesser Golden Plover usually hang around until November, while the Upland and Buff-breasted Sandpipers continue southward.

Many sandpiper species can be expected during the fall migration. Most of the "peep"—smallest of the sandpipers—cover Cape May in good numbers. Semipalmated, Least, and to a lesser degree Western and White-rumped Sandpipers have all arrived by September. Both Yellowlegs, with the Lesser the more abundant, frequent the mudflats in and around the park's ponds. Also present are Killdeer and Semipalmated, Black-bellied (now in white winter plumage), Piping (which prefers the beach front to all other habitats), and Lesser Golden Plovers. Sanderlings play with the waves while Ruddy Turnstones characteristically turn over shells in search of food and Short-billed Dowitchers rapidly probe the mudflats. Willets are always making a vocal commotion, and Spotted Sandpipers can be seen teeter-tottering. Dunlin have begun to arrive and will stay through the winter. Among the more uncommon species that occur singly or in small numbers are: Whimbrel, Red Knot, Common Snipe, and more and more frequently Wilson's and Northern Phalaropes. American Woodcock come to Cape May in sizable numbers, but, like many passerines, they migrate at night. About the first week in November, look for American Woodcock in densely covered swampy areas like those near the railroad tracks halfway between the point and Higbee Beach. Or check any damp hedgerow in the vicinity that borders open fields. Also good are the wooded bogs along both sides of the Parkway on the way to Cape May.

The fall landbird migration at Cape May is the most striking of all because of the sheer concentration of birds. This is especially true on days when many species accumulate while waiting for the right wind conditions to cross treacherous Delaware Bay. Anywhere around Cape May Point can be rewarding for the fall landbird migration, especially the brushy thickets of plum and grapevine, the hedgerows, and the pines and deciduous woodlots surrounding Lily Lake. Even birding along the streets to the lighthouse brings astonishing results. Higbee Beach is one of the less spoiled spots in the area, and offers great opportunities. The scrubby dunes of the beach are backed up by successional stands of pine, cedar, and oak, including dense growths of bayberry and briers of assorted species. Be careful of poison ivy here. Also make a point to walk along the railroad tracks already mentioned, for they traverse a variety of habitats.

What amazes everyone is the number of Common (Yellow-shafted) Flickers that pass through Cape May in late September. Many counts have shown thirty to fifty Flickers *per minute* crossing the checkpoint. Downy Woodpeckers and, less commonly, Yellow-bellied Sapsuckers are found in the thickets around the point. Gray Catbirds, Northern Mockingbirds, and Brown Thrashers mob the low shrubbery. Few flycatchers, except for the abundant Eastern Kingbird, are seen here.

In mid-September, droves of swallows have arrived and are swarming telephone wires, roads, and the sky. By far the most common are Tree Swallows, which come as early as August. Following in abundance are Barn, Bank, and Rough-winged Swallows (the last in early September), Purple Martin, and an occasional Cliff Swallow.

Common Nighthawk and Chimney Swift are better seen later in the afternoon. Other common species include American Robin, Blue Jay, American (Common) Crow, Fish Crow, Carolina Chickadee, Tufted Titmouse, Northern Cardinal, and White- and Red-breasted Nuthatches. Listen for the Marsh (Long-billed Marsh) Wren near the lighthouse pond and the Carolina and House Wrens in the wooded thickets. Walking the park's three color-marked hiking trails, red (one-half mile), blue (two miles), and yellow (just over one mile), will take you through the brackish marsh and the woodland habitat. Consisting of holly, maple, sweet gum, spanish oak, and various vine-like growths, these trails afford good birding possibilities. Besides the species already mentioned, look for the Hermit Thrush, which sometimes will winter here, and the abundant Swainson's (Olive-backed) Thrush. Common Bobwhite will probably be flushed somewhere along the trails. Yellow-billed and occasionally Black-billed Cuckoos sit high in the trees on these quiet trails. Both Ruby-crowned and Golden-crowned Kinglets commonly flit about with groups of chickadees. Blue-gray Gnatcatchers are seen up until late September, and Cedar Waxwings, when not feasting on insects, gorge themselves on the abundant berry bushes.

Warblers and vireos migrate through Cape May from late August through early October. Over twenty species of warblers are probable. The wooded thickets in and around the park, along with Higbee Beach and the railroad tracks, should produce the most species. Black-and-white, Northern Parula, Nashville, Yellow, Magnolia, Yellow-rumped (Myrtle), Black-throated Blue, Black-throated Green, Blackburnian, Pine, Prairie, Palm, Blackpoll, Ovenbird, Common Yellowthroat, American Redstart, Northern Waterthrush, Blue-winged, Chestnut-sided, Canada, and Tennessee Warblers and a few others should be expected. A little less widespread than the warblers, vireos are represented by the Red-eyed and (less frequently) the White-eyed and Solitary.

Five species of blackbirds populate the area in the fall. Common

Grackle, Brown-headed Cowbird, Red-winged and Rusty Black-birds, and Boat-tailed Grackle all stay near the marshes; the Brown-headed Cowbird is especially common in pastures. Bobolink, in its "reed-bird" plumage, and Eastern Meadowlark prefer the marshes of the point and old fields in the area. Bobolinks are very common on days with northwest winds and congregate in these places while waiting for the wind to shift for safe passage across the bay. Other common fall migrants include Rose-breasted Grosbeak, Northern (Baltimore) Oriole (until late September), American Goldfinch, Rufous-sided Towhee, and a number of sparrows. Savannah Sparrows have arrived by mid-September and a few of the Ipswich race can be found later in the winter. Both Sea-side and Sharp-tailed Sparrows wander in the point's salt meadows. Dark-eyed (Slate-colored) Juncos come in early October and remain for the winter months. Chipping Sparrows can be seen by walking the roads around the residential section near Lily Lake. Field, White-throated, and Song Sparrows forage in brushy open fields, while the Swamp and Fox Sparrows are best found in the wooded thickets around the ponds and along the color-marked hiking trails. The American Tree Sparrow is a winter bird and doesn't appear at Cape May until mid-November.

While many of the species mentioned winter at Cape May, other important winter birds don't appear until late October or November. Mid-November through December is an excellent time for a winter census; the D.V.O.C. typically picks the week surrounding Christmas for its annual Christmas Count. September and October hold hope for only a few early-winter stragglers.

For your winter tour, start as before with a scope and tripod near the defense base and scan the ocean. Red-throated Loons and Horned Grebes commonly float and dive. Common Loons do occur here, but in much smaller numbers than the Red-throated. The ratio of Red-throated to Common Loons can be reliably stated at 10:1. Be sure of the features that distinguish these two before identifying them. Flocks of Brant are intermittently swimming by, while the Snow Goose prefers the fresh-water ponds. Up to 10,400 Brant were seen on the 1974 Christmas Count; the numbers are similar each year. Small numbers of Canvasback, Ring-necked Duck, and the stiff-tailed Ruddy Duck occur every winter season. Bufflehead, Oldsquaw, and Greater and Lesser Scaup are now appearing in greater numbers. By early November, Northern Gannets have come southward. Setting your scope on one point on the horizon and waiting for the Northern Gannet to fly by the field of vision is the best way to spot it. The chances of seeing Northern Gannets will be greater on days with easterly winds, because they are then blown inland a little.

The Common Goldeneye is at home on both fresh and salt water and can usually be found in small numbers. Two Mergansers—Red-breasted and Hooded—occur regularly in winter, with the Red-breasted the more abundant of the two. The Red-breasted is typically a salt-water bird, while the Hooded is content on fresh water. Do not expect to see Common Mergansers regularly. Members of the Eider family, the King and Common, have been found at the Cape in single-digit numbers in wintertime. These two like shallow water, especially near the defense base and the jetties that dot the coast on either edge of the park.

While checking the water near the jetties, look for the rather tame Purple Sandpiper, which is common at this time of year, having arrived to winter by mid- to late November. Good numbers are present every season (including 388 in 1975).

Finding owls is difficult during the winter season. The wooded sections hold hope for both Common Screech and Great Horned Owls, while the day-flying Short-eared Owl is more easily spotted in the open areas around the park. The Christmas Count has reported small numbers each year for all three species. Horned Larks make their entrance by November 1 and frequent the low weedy fields and occasionally the grassy sand dunes. Also be on the lookout for Water Pipits in these same habitats. Finches come by in erratic groups. The resident House Finch is the most common; 450 were tallied in 1975, while their traditional eastern counterpart, the Purple Finch, is many years seen only in single digits. Small flocks of Evening Grosbeaks, usually less than fifty, appear every year. Pine Siskins are sporadic: some years several flocks will be seen, other years none. The snow bird of the winter season, the Snow Bunting, is also a nomadic species; however, it has missed the Christmas Count only a few years. Look for these now brown and dull, whitish birds on the grassy dunes of the park picking at weed seeds. In 1976, a good year, the Christmas Count recorded 300 individuals. When you discover a flock of Snow Buntings, carefully scan it for a different looking bird. This will likely be a Lapland Longspur, which is commonly known to fraternize with the Snow Buntings. Usually only single birds have been identified with a flock, but a high of seven was seen in one flock in 1973.

Cape May also has a reputation for attracting accidental species. Wood Stork (Ibis) and White Ibis occasionally turn up at the point, and the last few years have seen the regular appearance of the Western Kingbird in the fall. Other possibilities include Swallow-tailed and Mississippi Kites during the warmer months, and some wintering rarities such as Dovekie, Thin-billed (Common) and Thick-billed Murres, Black-legged Kittiwake, Harlequin Duck, and Red-necked Grebe. Other rarities, especially in early fall, include Purple Gallinule, Loggerhead Shrike, Lark Sparrow, Clay-colored Sparrow, Dickcissel, Yellow-headed Blackbird, and Fulvous Tree Duck. If in the area during the spring breeding season, stop at Cape May County Courthouse on your way to the point. This is the most reliable spot in the region to see breeding Red-headed Woodpeckers. As many as five breeding pairs have been found nesting in one season.

Birding at Cape May Point during the fall migration can be described quite simply. Wait for the northwest winds to come, and then be ready to not take the binoculars from your eyes.

For more information, and the park's birdlist, write:

Cape May Point State Park	Cape May Bird Observatory
Box 107	Box 3
Cape May Point, N.J. 08212	Cape May Point, N.J. 08212
Phone: (609) 884-2159	Phone: (609) 884-2736

Directions to Cape May Point State Park

To reach Cape May Point State Park, follow the directions to Brigantine National Wildlife Refuge. From the entrance to the Atlantic City Expressway drive 26.6 miles to the Egg Harbor toll booth. After paying the toll ($1.00 in 1979), travel 9.9 miles further on the expressway to Exit 7 South for the Garden State Parkway and Cape May. Drive 37.5 miles along the Garden State Parkway South to Route 109 South. Continue straight across the bridge on Route 109 South to Cape May. After crossing the bridge drive straight through the town of Cape May on Lafayette Street (2.1 miles). Bear right onto Perry Street at the

stop sign. At the light 0.4 miles further, Perry Street becomes Sunset Blvd. at the intersection with Broadway Street. Pass through this intersection and continue on Sunset Blvd. for 1.8 miles. Turn left between two stone pillars onto Cape Avenue. Lily Lake is just after the left onto Cape Avenue. To reach Cape May Point State Park, turn left immediately after turning onto Cape Avenue for fifty yards, then turn right onto Lighthouse Avenue. Drive 0.7 miles along Lighthouse Avenue, and the entrance to the state park is on your left.

A trip to Higbee Beach is worthwhile after birding the point. Exit between the two pillars and turn right onto Sunset Blvd. Drive 1.1 miles on Sunset Blvd., then make a left onto Bayshore Road. Travel 1.8 miles on Bayshore Road to the first major intersection. At the stop sign make a left and drive 1.2 miles to the earthen parking lot at Higbee Beach. Several trails radiate from the lot through the woods to the beach. It is best to walk these trails, as a car is likely to be swallowed up by the sands. A one-way trip to Cape May Point from Philadelphia takes approximately two hours.

Map 11
Directions to Cape May Point State Park

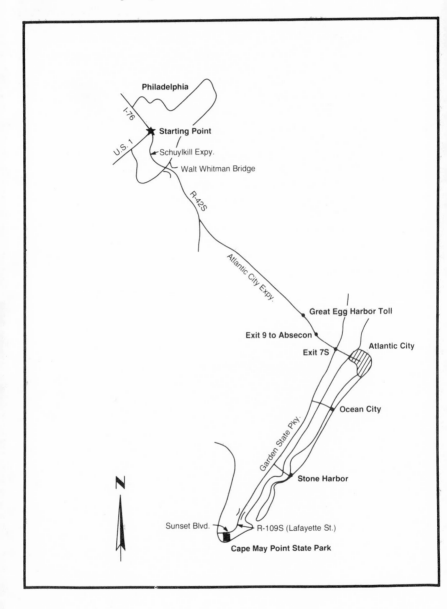

Map 12
Cape May Point State Park

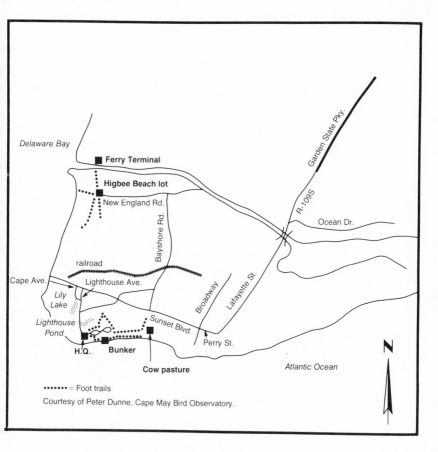

Delaware Bay

Ferry Terminal

Higbee Beach lot

New England Rd.

Bayshore Rd.

Garden State Pky.

R-109S

Ocean Dr.

railroad

Cape Ave.

Lighthouse Ave.

Lily Lake

Broadway

Lafayette St.

Lighthouse Pond

Sunset Blvd.

H.Q.   Bunker

Perry St.

Cow pasture

Atlantic Ocean

N

•••••• = Foot trails
Courtesy of Peter Dunne, Cape May Bird Observatory.

Bombay Hook
National Wildlife Refuge,
Little Creek Wildlife Area,
and Port Mahon,
Delaware

Bombay Hook National Wildlife Refuge

Bombay Hook National Wildlife Refuge, located ten miles northeast of Dover, Delaware, was established in 1937 for the protection of waterfowl along the Atlantic flyway. This 16,280-acre refuge lies along the western shore of Delaware Bay and consists mostly of salt-water marshes and tidal channels. Several fresh-water impoundments (covering 1,200 acres) serve as feeding areas for migratory waterfowl and shorebirds, while brushy, timbered swamps add a unique dimension to the various water habitats. One thousand acres of cropland provide forage for migrating Canada Geese, which peak at 35,000 during November. Large stands of deciduous hardwoods alternating with grassy meadows round out the preserve's wildlife environments.

Bombay Hook rivals Brigantine for the second-largest number of species after Cape May. Two hundred sixty-one different species are on Bombay Hook's checklist; another fifty species of accidental occurrence have also been recorded. Although the spring and fall migrations are best for seeing the greatest number of birds, any season provides exciting birding. Over one hundred species (designated † after the name) have nested on the refuge or in the immediate area, including several typical southern birds at their northern breeding limit. Using Bombay Hook as its center, the 1977 Christmas Count totaled 137 species.

Like Brigantine, Bombay Hook attracts large contingents of waterfowl and shorebirds. Brigantine is probably better for sheer numbers of birds concentrated in its two major impoundments. Also, Brigantine has more extensive salt-water areas within its boundaries that cater to seafowl. But as birding has rapidly grown at Bombay Hook over the past few years, it has become apparent that a greater variety of shorebirds visit Bombay Hook and the nearby Port Mahon–Little Creek preserves. This phenomenon will be discussed in detail later. Although many landbirds can be seen at Brigantine, its undiversified pine-oak woodlands limit the variety of potential nesters. Bombay Hook's deciduous forests, swamps, meadows, and croplands attract a greater selection of upland species. Bombay Hook and the Little Creek Wildlife Area are the northern breeding limit for Black-necked Stilt,† Black Vulture,† Prothonotary Warbler,† and Boat-tailed Grackle† in the region, although the latter two species have also established small colonies in New Jersey.

An extensive auto tour—nearly ten miles of gravel dikes and country dirt roads—samples all the preserve's representative habitats. Immediately after the headquarters the tour route is one-way around Raymond Pool, which is situated off to the left. After bearing right for a short distance, you continue by the vast Shearness Pool to the left. This mile-and-a-half stretch is open to two-way traffic, so drive carefully. Both Raymond and Shearness Pools are large fresh-water impoundments that attract migrating waterfowl and shorebirds. Both pools, although bordered by marsh vegetation and woods, seem more like open lakes. The dike road hugs the eastern border of these impoundments, providing excellent birding right from the road. Observation towers are found at each of Bombay Hook's pools except Finis Pool. To the right of the tour route are expansive salt-water meadows crisscrossed by a myriad of tidal channels.

After Shearness Pool, turn right onto the one-way dirt road around Bear Swamp Pool. Usually this pool is actually a brushy swamp. The back half of the loop around Bear Swamp Pool courses through hardwood stands alternating with open meadows. Back on the main route, bear right and continue on for approximately one mile to the historic Allee House. Meadows, cultivated fields, and second-growth hedgerows host upland birds not seen along the impoundments.

Turn around in the Allee House parking lot and, after approximately three-quarters of a mile, make a right onto the Finis Pool road. Mixed hardwoods border the road to the left; many typical eastern landbirds breed in this area. After three-quarters of a mile this dirt road crosses Finis Pool—an extensive timbered swamp whose slow-moving waters feed Shearness Pool. Park your car in the cul-de-sac by the gate and walk back along the dike road through the swamp. Or you can pass under the gate and walk straight ahead several hundred yards under the drier forest canopy. After birding, head back to the headquarters—past Finis Pool, the woodlands, and Shearness and Raymond Pools. Bear right at all possible turns and crossroads.

As mentioned before, spring and fall migrations provide the greatest birdwatching opportunities, although the recent Christmas Count of nearly 140 species proves that any season can be rewarding. The Delaware Valley Birding Hot Line, at (215) 567-BIRD, covers the more exciting species seen the week before. Before starting your tour, stop by the visitors' center near the headquarters to check the weekly update of sightings.

A birding scope is essential. Most birdwatching can be done right from the network of dikes and roads. Seasonal clothing (summer: 75°– 90° F; winter: 25°– 45° F) and insect repellent (June through September) make life easier. While the auto tour can be blitzed in under two hours, it's best to spend the entire day. Include a side trip to the nearby Port Mahon–Little Creek area, which will be discussed later.

In March, Raymond and Shearness Pools and the adjacent saltwater marshes come alive as staging areas for the spring waterfowl migration. Many species will remain in fewer numbers to breed, although several species have virtually disappeared as summer nesters over the past decade. Good concentrations of Canada Goose,† Snow Goose, Mallard,† American Black Duck,† Gadwall,† Common Pintail, Green- and Blue-winged† Teals, American Wigeon, Northern Shoveler,† Ring-necked Duck, Greater and Lesser Scaup, Bufflehead, Ruddy Duck,† and American Coot† are to be expected during the early spring. Smaller numbers of Horned and Pied-billed† Grebes, Whistling Swan, Wood Duck,† Canvasback, and Common and Hooded Mergansers are also present. Other waterfowl listed are only occasional. Most are seafowl or diving ducks, which are not likely to be seen on the refuge proper as Bombay Hook has little open salt water. Seafowl would include Common and Red-throated Loons, Horned Grebe, Brant, Redhead, Canvasback, Greater Scaup, Common Goldeneye, Bufflehead, Oldsquaw, the Scoter family, and Red-breasted Merganser. Head toward Delaware Bay (i.e., Port Mahon) to add these birds to your list.

A pair of Bald Eagles† breed at Bombay Hook each year. By March, these birds are incubating on their massive nest. Look for them patrolling Shearness Pool; their nest is often concealed in the heavy timber of Parson Point, which juts out into this vast impoundment.

Several Owls, including Barn,† Common Screech,† Great Horned,† and Barred,† nest in their appropriate habitats, but must usually be "called in" at night. The start of the various owls' breeding periods varies with the species—from as early as late January for the Great Horned† to as late as April for the Common Screech.† The Short-eared Owl,† while still a common winter visitor, probably no longer breeds on or near the refuge. Bombay Hook (especially Finis Pool) and the marshy woodlands along the way to the nearby Woodland Beach Wildlife Area are the best spots in the region to find the Barred Owl.† The four nesting owls are present year-round.

By mid-April, the wading-bird contingent is well represented. Great Blue Heron,† Great† (Common) and Snowy† Egrets, Black-crowned Night Heron,† and Glossy Ibis† are common along the impoundments. Little Blue† and Louisiana† Herons are less frequent at the refuge, while the Yellow-crowned Night Heron visits only rarely. The Green Heron† is common along the timbered, swampy edges of Finis Pool, while the Cattle Egret† is regularly observed working the pastures along Road 85 toward the refuge. Least† and American† Bitterns nest among the reeds surrounding the pools, but are difficult to glimpse. Most of the above birds can also be found, sometimes in large breeding colonies, at Little Creek, approximately fourteen car miles south of the refuge. Little Creek is also the northernmost breeding locale for the Black-necked Stilt.†

Early May heralds the impressive shorebird migration. American Woodcock† and Common Snipe have long since arrived and are found along the swampy wooded edges of the preserve. Semipalmated Plover, Killdeer,† Black-bellied Plover, Whimbrel, Spotted Sandpiper, Willet,† Greater and Lesser Yellowlegs, Dunlin, Short-billed Dowitcher, Least and Semipalmated Sandpipers, and Sanderling frequent the pools' muddy borders and the adjoining tidal flats. Ruddy Turnstone, Solitary Sandpiper, Red Knot, and Pectoral and (in early June) White-rumped Sandpipers are occasionally seen. Each May, certain rarer species visit Bombay Hook's impoundments, usually in singles. Lesser (American) Golden Plover, Ruff, Wilson's and Northern Phalaropes, and the extremely rare Curlew Sandpiper have been reported. The extensive Port Mahon–Little Creek impoundments are even more likely spots for these exciting occurrences.

The secretive King† and Virginia† Rails and Sora† are common in the fresh and brackish marshes during May, but they are seldom observed. Fewer numbers remain to breed during the summer months. The Common Gallinule† works the pools' vegetation, while the furtive Clapper Rail† darts along the tidal flats to the right of the dike road. In past years a pair of Purple Gallinules† nested at Dragon Run Marsh, Delaware City, Delaware (north of Bombay Hook). This bird should be looked for at the refuge, and, indeed, a breeding pair has been present some years at Bombay Hook.

While circling the dikes and country roads, look for birds overhead. Osprey† nest every year near the refuge, as do Turkey Vulture,† American Kestrel† (Sparrow Hawk), and an occasional Black Vulture.† Although listed as breeders, the Red-tailed† and Red-shouldered† Hawks and Northern Harrier† (Marsh Hawk) have practically disappeared as summer residents over the past decade. Various gulls and terns, including the transient Bonaparte's Gull and Black Tern, are also seen over the impoundments.

Early to mid-May also brings the major landbird movement. As mentioned before, the woodlots, hedgerows, and meadows cater to a large number of both migrating and breeding species. The road leading to Finis Pool is excellent, as are the several trails radiating from the Finis Pool cul-de-sac. The meadows and hedgerows along the Allee House Road (Dutch Neck Road) are also rewarding— especially near their junction with the woods beyond.

All eastern thrushes, except the Eastern Bluebird, are common during spring migration. Of the vireos, the Red-eyed† and White-eyed† are most likely to be seen, although the Solitary and Yellow-throated† Vireos are also listed. At least eighteen species of warblers are frequently observed during the spring migration: Black-and-white, Northern Parula, Yellow,† Magnolia, Black-throated Blue, Yellow-rumped (Myrtle), Black-throated Green,

Chestnut-sided, Blackpoll, and Palm Warblers, Ovenbird,† Northern and Louisiana† Waterthrushes, Kentucky Warbler,† Common Yellowthroat,† Yellow-breasted Chat,† Canada Warbler, and American Redstart.† Of these, the Yellow Warbler,† Myrtle Warbler, and Common Yellowthroat† are ubiquitous. An additional dozen or so warbler species are occasionally seen. The Prothonotary Warbler,† a typical southerner, breeds annually at Bombay Hook, although in very small numbers. The favorite location seems to be along the marshy borders of Finis Pool. At the cul-de-sac, pass under the gate and follow the trail along the pool off to the left. Listen here for the characteristic notes of the Prothonotary; the adjacent dense woods harbor nesting Kentucky† and, rarely, Hooded† Warblers.

May is a transition month for birding. In addition to migrants, summering birds begin nesting. Various breeding members of the woodpecker, flycatcher, swallow, wren, blackbird, oriole, finch, and sparrow families are likely to be seen during a spring trip and will be discussed shortly.

June, with its biting flies and mosquitoes, marks the beginning of summer at Bombay Hook. Broods of ducks and geese venture out onto the fresh-water impoundments, while the nesting boxes along Finis Pool house Wood Ducks.† Various herons, egrets, bitterns, and rails already mentioned nest on the preserve or in nearby rookeries. Common Gallinule,† Killdeer,† Willet,† and an occasional American Coot† are the common marsh breeders, while Common Bobwhite† and Ring-necked Pheasant† favor the open meadows and croplands. Greater Black-backed, Herring, Ring-billed, and Laughing Gulls are common, especially closer to Delaware Bay. Forster's† and Little† (Least) Terns are frequently seen at the refuge, while the Gull-billed† and Common† Terns and Black Skimmer† are more regular in the Port Mahon–Little Creek area.

The refuge's deciduous woodlands, typical of the eastern United States, host many nesting species. Yellow-billed† and occasionally Black-billed† Cuckoos, Common (Yellow-shafted) Flicker,† Red-bellied Woodpecker,† Hairy† and Downy† Woodpeckers, Great Crested Flycatcher,† Eastern Phoebe,† Acadian Flycatcher,† Eastern (Wood) Pewee,† Blue Jay,† Carolina Chickadee,† Tufted Titmouse,† Carolina Wren,† American Robin,† Wood Thrush,† Blue-gray Gnatcatcher,† Red-eyed Vireo,† Ovenbird,†

Kentucky Warbler,† American Redstart,† Scarlet Tanager,† and Rufous-sided Towhee† are commonly observed or heard singing. Several other species breed in the woodlands, but are much less frequently seen. Check the refuge birdlist.

The more open second-growth areas, thickets, and brushy hedgerows attract a different clientele. Eastern Kingbird,† House Wren,† Northern Mockingbird,† Gray Catbird,† Brown Thrasher,† White-eyed Vireo,† Yellow Warbler,† Common Yellowthroat,† Yellow-breasted Chat,† Northern Cardinal,† Blue Grosbeak,† Indigo Bunting,† American Goldfinch,† and Chipping,† Field,† Swamp,† and Song† Sparrows are common here. Willow ("Fitz-Bew") Flycatcher† and Orchard† and rarely Northern (Baltimore) Orioles have also been noted.

Extensive rolling meadows and cultivated fields bordered by brushy drainage ditches are found behind Bear Swamp Pool and especially along the road to the Allee House. Killdeer,† an occasional Horned Lark,† Eastern Meadowlark,† Red-winged Blackbird,† Common Grackle,† Brown-headed Cowbird,† and Grasshopper† and Song† Sparrows occur here in summer. Blue Grosbeaks† working the hedgerows and Grasshopper Sparrows† buzzing from the adjoining fields are a rewarding combination that is frequently seen along the Allee House Road. Although it is rarely seen nowadays, this is also good habitat for Henslow's Sparrow.

The Marsh (Long-billed Marsh) Wren† frequents the reeds and cattail stands around the impoundments. The Sedge (Short-billed Marsh) Wren† is a rare, irregular nester in the sedge meadows. A probable breeding pair of Sedge Wrens† was present at Bear Swamp Pool during the summer of 1977. This latter wren is more reliable (although still irregular) in the short-grass meadows lining the roads through Prime Hook National Wildlife Refuge, twenty-five miles south of Bombay Hook. Red-winged Blackbird† and Sharp-tailed† and Seaside† Sparrows are commonly found in the salt marshes of the refuge and in the boggy Bear Swamp Pool. Bombay Hook is one of the northernmost breeding limits for the Boat-tailed Grackle,† which is usually seen closer to the Delaware Bay and Little Creek.

The swallow family rounds out the summer contingent of land birds. Although found everywhere on the preserve, swallows seem most concentrated along the wires near headquarters and the Allee House. Chimney Swift, Tree,† Bank, and Barn† Swallows, and

Purple Martin† abound, while Rough-winged and Cliff Swallows are occasional migrants.

August marks the height of the fall shorebird migration, which runs from late July through early October. Raymond, Shearness, and Bear Swamp Pools attract large numbers of southbound migrants, especially if water levels are low. A visit to the Little Creek Wildlife Area is particularly worthwhile now. This vast complex of mud flats and wading pools literally crawls with shorebirds. Little Creek also swarms with herons, egrets, and terns.

All the spring migrants already mentioned return in even greater numbers during the autumn movement. In addition, Pectoral, White-rumped, Stilt, and Western Sandpipers are regularly seen each fall at both Bombay Hook and Little Creek. Wilson's and Northern Phalaropes come in drifts. Marbled and Hudsonian Godwits and the Ruff are more likely to occur from late July through September than at other times. Search the freshly plowed fields along Road 85 near the refuge for Lesser Golden Plover, which may be almost common in early September. Large contingents of American Avocet, up to one hundred birds, visit Raymond and Shearness Pools from August through October. Be on the lookout for Whistling (Fulvous Tree) Duck—practically every year a few stray into Bombay Hook during the late summer. The pair of Common Shelducks that have visited Bombay Hook for the past several years are escapees from a nearby aviary.

Labor Day signals the frenzied beginning of the fall landbird migration. This is an excellent time to visit Bombay Hook as the shorebird movement is still in full tilt. Most spring transients also appear in autumn—often in confusing fall plumages. Bobolinks are frequently seen during September, having returned from their northern breeding grounds. Other species that are more common in fall begin to trickle in, including Rusty Blackbird and Savannah and Fox Sparrows—although the Rusty Blackbird and Fox Sparrow don't arrive until mid-October.

Raptor flights are less than spectacular at Bombay Hook. Visit Cape May and Hawk Mountain for the autumn hawk migration. October welcomes the buildup of Canada Geese† and ducks on the refuge's impoundments.

Winter sneaks quietly into Bombay Hook during November. Good flights of Snow Geese join the massing army of Canada Geese,† which peaks at over 30,000 around Thanksgiving. The

Whistling Swan is regularly seen in small numbers at this time, especially in the open waters of Raymond and Shearness Pools. Each year, single Greater White-fronted Geese are reported among the large flocks of Canada Geese† in the area.

Duck concentrations rapidly increase during November, with many species wintering over on the refuge. All the ducks present during the spring migration return in even greater numbers during the fall movement. Check the huge rafts of Green-winged Teal for a lone Common (European) Teal, and be on the lookout for a Eurasian (European) Wigeon among the American Wigeons from November through March. A few Brant are usually found on the Delaware Bay (Port Mahon), as are other seafowl.

Great Blue Heron,† Killdeer,† and Dunlin are the only shore-birds to be reliably expected during the coldest months. Great Egret,† Black-crowned Night Heron,† American Bittern,† Clap-per† and Virginia† Rails, Black-bellied Plover, Common Snipe, Greater and Lesser Yellowlegs, and various sandpipers are some-times encountered. Greater Black-backed, Herring, and Ring-billed Gulls are common during the winter, while the Bonaparte's Gull is occasionally seen, especially at Port Mahon during the early spring.

Other than waterfowl, birds of prey are the winter birding at-traction at Bombay Hook. Bald Eagles† can often be seen patrol-ling Shearness Pool awaiting their February nesting start. Rarely, a Golden Eagle visits the refuge during this period. Red-tailed Hawk,† American Kestrel,† and infrequently the Red-shouldered Hawk† are also seen. Bombay Hook is one of the most promising locations to view the Rough-legged Hawk, Northern Harrier,† and Short-eared Owl.† Search for them quartering the vast salt marshes of the refuge and along the meadows toward the Allee House. Scan the horizon for the occasional Black Vulture† among the more common Turkey Vultures.† Delaware is the northern-most area where the Black Vulture† can reliably be found, espe-cially during the colder months.

The woodlands are relatively quiet from November through March. Basically the same fare of landbirds is seen at Bombay Hook as at Brigantine. Red-bellied Woodpecker† (rare at Brig-antine), Hairy† and Downy† Woodpeckers, Blue Jay,† both Chickadees, Tufted Titmouse,† White-breasted Nuthatch, Brown Creeper, Carolina Wren,† American Robin,† Hermit Thrush,

Golden-crowned and Ruby-crowned Kinglets, Rusty Blackbird, Common Grackle,† and White-throated and Fox Sparrows are common. The Carolina Chickadee† far outnumbers the Black-capped at Bombay Hook during the winter; just the opposite holds true north of Philadelphia. Several other species, including Yellow-bellied Sapsucker, Red-breasted Nuthatch, and Winter Wren, are occasionally seen.

Northern Mockingbird,† Myrtle Warbler, Northern Cardinal,† American Goldfinch,† Dark-eyed (Slate-colored) Junco, and American Tree, Field,† Swamp,† and Song† Sparrows frequent the hedgerows and brushy meadows. Be on the lookout for the Loggerhead Shrike, which favors the exposed branches of the hedgerows' scattered trees. This bird is recorded every year on the local Christmas Count. Bombay Hook is perhaps the most reliable spot in the region to see this winter visitor. Eastern Meadowlark,† Red-winged Blackbird,† Common Grackle,† Brown-headed Cowbird,† Savannah Sparrow, and an occasional Sharp-tailed Sparrow† frequent the salt marshes and open upland areas. Over the past few years, good numbers of wintering Boat-tailed Grackles† have been tallied in the salt marshes of Bombay Hook and the Little Creek Wildlife Area. Horned Lark† and Water Pipit work the plowed fields and corn stubble along Road 85, although most pipits have passed through by December. Look for these winter vagrants: Evening Grosbeak, Purple Finch, and Pine Siskin in the woodlands, White-crowned and Vesper Sparrows along the hedgerows, and Snow Bunting and Lapland Longspur gleaning the open fields.

Little Creek Wildlife Area

Any birding trip to Bombay Hook should include a visit to the Little Creek Wildlife Area. Migrating shorebirds, waders, and certain "specialty" birds are more plentiful here than at Bombay Hook. Less than fourteen car miles south of the refuge, this 3,900-acre preserve can be driven to in twenty minutes. Two vast freshwater impoundments, separated by a north-south dike, are the main attraction.

Much of the time, especially during late summer, when water levels are low, Little Creek's East Pool is a quiltwork of extensive mudflats, potholes, and small vegetated islands. The smaller West

Pool is more of a shallow lake. From the earthen parking lot at the corner of the two impoundments (Pickering Beach access), you can walk the north dike for several hundred yards. Peering through the reeds at intervals affords a panoramic view of both pools. Spring and late summer provide the greatest concentrations and number of species, especially waders, shorebirds, and terns. A good zoom scope is necessary for adequate coverage.

The Pickering Beach access is the most popular. From the Bombay Hook headquarters, travel back 2.7 miles along Road 85 to Route 9. Make a left onto Route 9 South and drive 10.6 miles through and past the town of Little Creek. At the prominent sign for Pickering Beach, turn left onto Road 349 and go another 1.6 miles to the Little Creek Wildlife Area sign. Make a left onto the narrow gravel road by the dilapidated houses and wind around 0.4 miles to the earthen parking lot. An observation tower at the far end of the pool can be reached by driving back 0.8 miles on Route 9 North toward the town of Little Creek. Make a right at the almost hidden sign for the Little Creek Wildlife Area and follow the one-lane dirt road for another 1.2 miles to the tower.

Herons, egrets, bitterns, and rails are common at Little Creek, and certain species have large breeding colonies here. This is the northernmost location for nesting Black-necked Stilt.† Gull-billed,† Forster's,† Common,† and Little† Terns and Black Skimmer† breed at Little Creek or nearby coastal locales. For several years now, a White-winged Black Tern has been a late summer waif found among the common migrating Black Terns. All the spring and fall shorebirds found at Bombay Hook occur at Little Creek, often in greater numbers. Lesser Golden Plover, Stilt Sandpiper, Ruff, and Wilson's and Northern Phalaropes are regular August visitors. Hudsonian Godwit, American Avocet, and the accidental White Ibis are occasionally seen from late summer through fall. Nesting Boat-tailed Grackle† should also be looked for.

In some years during early summer (June), the Sedge Wren† can be found in the sedge meadows west of the dirt road leading from Road 349 to the parking lot. Common Screech,† Great Horned,† and Barred† Owls, Whip-poor-will,† and Henslow's Sparrow have also been heard along Road 349 during May. In winter, continue along Road 349 one mile past the Wildlife Area sign to Delaware Bay and search for seafowl.

Port Mahon

Nearby Port Mahon offers brackish pools, tidal marshes, and the Delaware Bay.

From the Bombay Hook headquarters, drive back 2.7 miles along Road 85 to Route 9. Make a left onto Route 9 South and travel 8 miles to the Little Creek Firehouse. Turn left just before the firehouse onto Road 89 (Port Mahon Road). At 0.9 miles, turn right onto a narrow gravel road that winds around for sixty yards to an earthen parking lot.

Here is a large fresh-water impoundment that is actually the northernmost extension of the Little Creek Wildlife Area. Its character and birdlife are similar to those of the other Little Creek pools.

Back on Road 89 (Port Mahon Road), travel another 2.2 miles past extensive tidal marshes on your left to a series of old wharfs on Delaware Bay. Scope the bay for diving ducks and other seafowl during the colder months. Each spring in recent years (March through early May), varying numbers of Little and less frequently Black-headed Gulls are reported from this area. In April 1975, more than thirty Little Gulls and several Black-headed Gulls were seen. These birds, along with the more common Bonaparte's Gull, range widely between the bay here and the nearby Little Creek pools.

Pig Farm

For the past twenty years or so, a small flock of Brewer's Blackbirds (up to two dozen birds) has wintered near Bombay Hook. Burrough's pig farm is a favorite location. Mixed flocks of European Starling,† Common Grackle,† Brown-headed Cowbird,† and Rusty and Brewer's Blackbirds are often seen in the feed lot from late November through March. Search the fields on either side of Road 326 for Lesser Golden Plover and Upland Sandpiper (Plover) during September. Horned Lark,† Water Pipit, and Snow Bunting are frequently seen during the colder months.

From the Bombay Hook headquarters, drive back 2.7 miles along Road 85 to Route 9. Make a left onto Route 9 North.

Several hundred yards later bear left onto Road 12 toward Smyrna (same route as coming to the refuge). At the second crossroads 1.3 miles along Road 12 make a left on Road 326. The pig pen is 0.4 miles further on the right.

For more information, and the refuge birdlist, write:

Bombay Hook National Wildlife
  Refuge
R.D. 1, Box 147
Smyrna, Del. 19977
Phone: (302) 653-9345

Directions to Bombay Hook National Wildlife Refuge

Only ten miles northeast of Dover, Delaware, Bombay Hook is within a sixty mile, one hour and forty-five minute drive of Philadelphia. Proceed as before to the Tinicum Preserve. Pass the turnoff to Tinicum at the Cobblestone Apartments, and continue straight on 84th Ave. for 0.65 miles to the dead end at the light. Make a right onto Bartram Avenue (following the signs for Interstate 95 South) and drive 1.6 miles to the first light. Bear right onto Route 291 West, travel 0.6 mile, and make another right onto I-95 South (a continuous one-half mile section linking Bartram Avenue and I-95 South is under construction). I-95 South can also be picked up at various points in Philadelphia, e.g., at the entrance to the Walt Whitman Bridge. Travel 22.3 miles along I-95 South, past Chester and Wilmington, to Exit 5 (sign for Route 13 Dover–Route 141 Newcastle). Drive 0.5 miles on the Exit 5 offramp and take the second cloverleaf for Route 13 South to Dover. Go another 2 miles, following the signs for Route 13 South, then make a right onto Route 13 South itself. Drive 28.2 miles along Route 13 South to the junction with Route 300 in Smyrna. Travel another 1.2 miles past this intersection and bear left onto Road 12 at the Bombay Hook N.W.R.–Leipsic sign. Go 4.85 miles along Road 12 to the sign for the Bombay Hook N.W.R. on Route 9 South (Road 12 turns into Route 9 South several hundred yards before the sign). Turn left at the refuge marker and drive another 2.7 miles on Road 85 to the headquarters.

Map 13
Directions to Bombay Hook National Wildlife Refuge

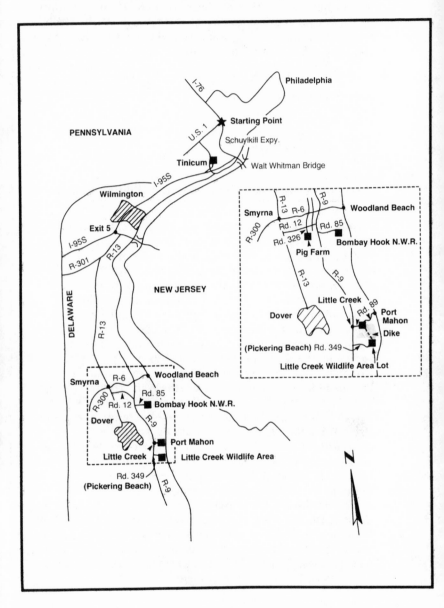

Map 14
Bombay Hook National Wildlife Refuge

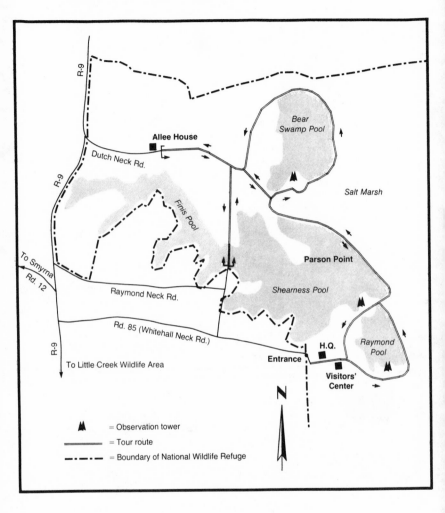

Other Birding Hot Spots in the Delaware Valley Region

Hot Spots

This section describes an additional nineteen birding hot spots to round out the coverage of the Delaware Valley region. These locations, while not as famous or all-inclusive as the six major refuges, provide the birder an opportunity to observe the area's representative species, plus the chance to see birds not found elsewhere. They are chosen for several reasons. Some, such as Wissahickon, Princeton, and Bowman's Hill, are noted for spring waves of landbird migrants. Others, like Barnegat Lighthouse, Ocean City, and Stone Harbor Sanctuary, cater to particular species seen only in limited habitat during the proper season. Certain spots, including the Pocono Mountains, Mercer Sod Farm, and the Pelagic Trips, allow the birder to see very local or specialized birds not likely to be encountered elsewhere in the region.

Each mini-chapter includes a general description of a particular hot spot, directions, and a brief résumé of the species likely to be seen. These areas are grouped according to state. Passing reference is made to another thirty-three locations at the end of the state groupings. These latter areas tend to be similar to the spots already described, and are included mainly because of their local interest.

Pennsylvania

Wissahickon Valley (Carpenter's Woods), Philadelphia

The Wissahickon Valley, a section of Philadelphia's Fairmount Park, extends approximately seven miles from the mouth of the Wissahickon Creek by the Schuylkill River northwestward to the city limit near Chestnut Hill College. The valley's main attraction is the slow-moving Wissahickon Creek, which courses through a large wooded ravine. The principal habitat is mixed deciduous hardwoods with scattered coniferous plantings, especially hemlock. A vast open scrubby area can be found in the northernmost section of the park, where Bells Mill Road crosses the creek. White-eyed Vireo, Yellow-breasted Chat, Orchard Oriole, Indigo Bunting, and American Goldfinch are frequently observed in this latter area during the breeding season.

The Wissahickon's migrating and resident birdlife is very similar to that of Ridley Creek. Carpenter's Woods, a famous birding hot spot of only several acres, branches off the Wissahickon Valley proper. Large numbers of migrating landbirds funnel through here during their spring and autumn movements.

At the light before the City Line Avenue entrance onto Interstate 76 East (Schuylkill Expressway), stay in the left lane. Follow the signs for Ridge Avenue, cross the bridge, and after 0.4 miles bear left again, following the signs for Wissahickon Drive. Travel 1.5 miles along Wissahickon Drive to the first light. Bear right onto Rittenhouse Place, following the signs for Wissahickon Avenue (Wissahickon Drive becomes Lincoln Drive along the way). Wind around 0.15 miles along Rittenhouse Place to the next light. Make a left onto Wissahickon Avenue (North). Drive 1.1 miles on Wissahickon Avenue past four traffic lights to Carpenter's Lane. Make a right onto Carpenter's Lane, drive another block (0.1 mile), and make a left onto Wayne Avenue. Continue on Wayne Avenue to the parking lot for Carpenter's Woods (0.1 mile further). This parking area is located at the intersection of Wayne and Sedgewick Avenues. A one-way trip takes approximately twenty minutes.

Both walking and bridle paths straddle Wissahickon Creek for almost its entire length—from the Schuylkill River to Chestnut Hill College. You can reach the scrubby Bells Mill area by walking these trails north for several miles past the Wissahickon Avenue junction with the creek. This area can also be reached directly by auto—consult the regional maps at the end of this chapter for exact directions.

The best times to visit the Wissahickon Valley, and especially Carpenter's Woods, are during the first three weeks in May and again in late August through mid-September. Unbelievable concentrations of woodpeckers, flycatchers, thrushes, vireos, warblers, orioles, fringillids, and sparrows pass through during spring migration. Warblers are the reason to visit Carpenter's Woods. The following species should be observed on at least half of the birding trips to the area during May († indicates species that have nested in the Wissahickon Valley area): Ruby-throated Humming-bird,† Common (Yellow-shafted) Flicker,† Red-bellied,† Hairy,† and Downy† Woodpeckers, Yellow-bellied Sapsucker (April), Eastern Kingbird,† Great Crested Flycatcher,† Eastern Phoebe,† Acadian Flycatcher,† Least Flycatcher, Eastern (Wood) Pewee,† Blue Jay,† both Chickadees (Carolina is local breeder), Tufted Titmouse,† White-breasted Nuthatch, Brown Creeper (April), House Wren,† Winter Wren (April), Carolina Wren,† Gray Cat-bird,† Brown Thrasher,† American Robin,† Wood Thrush,† Hermit Thrush (April), Swainson's (Olive-backed) and Gray-cheeked Thrushes, Veery,† Blue-gray Gnatcatcher,† Golden-crowned and Ruby-crowned Kinglets (April), Cedar Waxwing, Solitary Vireo (late April), Red-eyed Vireo,† Black-and-white, Blue-winged,† Tennessee, Northern Parula, Yellow,† Magnolia, Black-throated Blue, Black-throated Green, Yellow-rumped (Myrtle), Blackbur-nian, Chestnut-sided,† Bay-breasted, Blackpoll, and Palm (April) Warblers, Ovenbird,† Northern Waterthrush, Louisiana Water-thrush† (becoming scarce as a breeder), Kentucky Warbler† (more common elsewhere in the Wissahickon Valley), Common Yel-lowthroat,† Canada Warbler, American Redstart,† Northern (Baltimore) Oriole,† Scarlet Tanager,† Northern Cardinal,† Rose-breasted Grosbeak,† Rufous-sided Towhee,† Dark-eyed (Slate-colored) Junco (April), White-throated and Fox Sparrows (April), and Song Sparrow.†

Carpenter's Woods is especially good for migrating Cape May, Tennessee, and Bay-breasted Warblers—these birds are not particularly common elsewhere. The rarely seen Worm-eating, Golden-winged, Wilson's, Hooded,† and Cerulean† Warblers are recorded every year at Carpenter's Woods. The last two species have bred in the Wissahickon Valley; the Cerulean favors the tall trees adjoining the creek between the Covered Bridge (near Thomas Mill Road) and Bells Mill Road.

Special thanks to Mr. Stephen Lawrence for the use of the records that he has compiled over the past twenty years at Carpenter's Woods.

Map 15
Carpenter's Woods and Wissahickon Valley

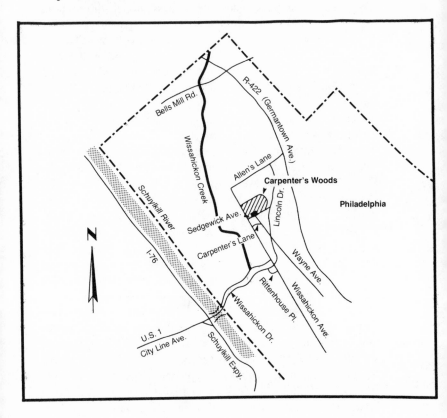

Struble Lake and King Ranch, Chester County

Struble Lake, in northwestern Chester County, is a large man-made impoundment recently developed by the Pennsylvania Fish and Game Commission. The surrounding countryside is typical of Chester County's fertile rolling farmlands—just outside the Philadelphia metropolitan area. This lake provides the inland birder with an opportunity to see waterfowl that are generally concentrated in more coastal locations.

From the intersection of Route 1 South (City Line Avenue) with Route 3 West (West Chester Pike), make a right onto Route 3 West and travel 15.3 miles to signs for Route 202 North and Route 322 West (bear right). This is immediately before the town of West Chester. Drive onto the entrance ramp for Route 202 and quickly—0.8 miles later—exit at the sign for Route 322 West to Downingtown to the right. Travel 8.1 miles on the winding Route 322 West to the center of Downingtown. At the light, make a hard left for 0.2 miles, then a hard right at the next light back onto Route 322 West. Drive another 6.9 miles along Route 322 West to the junction with Route 82. Go another 1.2 miles further on Route 322 West past the intersection and make a right onto Chestnut Tree Road at the sign for Struble Lake. This is the first right turn after the junction of Route 322 West and Route 82. Drive 2.6 miles along Chestnut Tree Road, then bear left at the sign for Struble Lake. The lake entrance is 0.5 miles further over the hill. A one-way trip generally takes one hour.

The most productive time to visit Struble Lake is during the colder months—October through April. Large concentrations of various waterfowl can be found on this huge impoundment, with peak numbers in November and late March. During these periods, Pied-billed and Horned Grebes, Canada Goose, Mallard, American Black Duck, Gadwall, Green-winged and Blue-winged Teals, American Wigeon, Northern Shoveler, Ring-necked Duck, Lesser Scaup, Bufflehead, and Ruddy Duck are likely to be seen. Less frequently observed are Whistling Swan, Snow and Blue Geese, Common Pintail, Wood Duck, Canvasback, Greater Scaup, Common Goldeneye, Hooded and Common Mergansers, and American Coot. Common and Red-throated Loons, Red-necked Grebe,

Greater White-fronted Goose, Redhead, Oldsquaw, and the scoter family have been occasionally recorded. In April 1978, a probable wild Barnacle Goose was found keeping company with a large flock of Canada Geese. Struble Lake is one of the most reliable locales in the region to see Ring-necked Duck, Lesser Scaup, and Canvasback during the colder months. Scan the lake's edge in May and late August for migrating shorebirds and loafing herons and egrets.

Search the winter countryside for patrolling raptors. Possibilities are American Kestrel (Sparrow Hawk), Red-tailed Hawk, Turkey Vulture, Northern Harrier (Marsh Hawk), and Rough-legged Hawk, in order of decreasing frequency. Vagrant Black Vultures and Loggerhead Shrike have also been seen in the general area.

From late August through September, large numbers of all swallows can be observed hawking insects over the lake. This is a good location to see the Rough-winged Swallow and the uncommon Cliff Swallow.

During late fall (mid-October through early December), Water Pipit, Horned Lark, Snow Bunting, and the rare Lapland Longspur work the plowed fields and corn stubble of the nearby farmlands. The adjoining hedgerows provide cover for various sparrows, including the White-crowned and the rarely seen Vesper Sparrow.

A side trip to the Unionville area can be worthwhile in spring and early summer (May–June).

After leaving Struble Lake, head back to Route 322 East. Travel 1.2 mile along Route 322 East and make a right onto Route 82 South. Drive through Coatesville and continue on Route 82 South to the section between Doe Run and Unionville, Pennsylvania.

This area is part of the King Ranch, with its rolling pastures, swampy grasslands, and scattered tree groves. Small breeding colonies of Savannah Sparrow and Bobolink have recently been discovered. Grasshopper Sparrow and the extremely rare Henslow's Sparrow have also been recorded in this general area. In recent years the Black Vulture has been observed year-round in southern Chester and Lancaster Counties. Scan the horizon over the King Ranch along Route 82 South to add this bird to your Big May Day and Christmas Count lists.

Map 16
Struble Lake and King Ranch

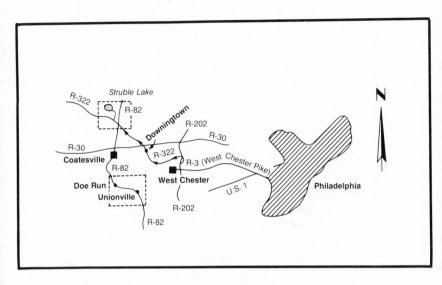

Map 17
Struble Lake

Map 18
King Ranch

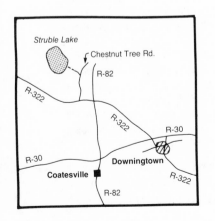

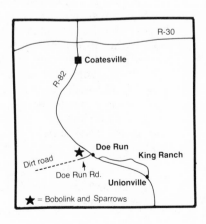

Bowman's Hill, Bucks County, and Bull's Island, Raven Rock

Bowman's Hill, a section of Washington Crossing State Park, is located in central Bucks County, just outside the Philadelphia metropolitan area. Two locales within the park—Bowman's Hill Tower and Bowman's Hill State Wildflower Preserve—are especially rewarding hot spots. Spring migrants and nesting woodland birds are this area's specialties. In addition, the wildflower preserve has a staffed headquarters and a well-marked network of trails coursing through one hundred acres of native American wildflower plantings. The general habitat and avifauna are similar to those found at Ridley Creek and Tyler Arboretum. Certain species nest here that only sporadically breed in more southern areas. Broad-winged Hawk, Pileated Woodpecker, Black-capped Chickadee, Worm-eating Warbler, Scarlet Tanager, and Rose-breasted Grosbeak regularly nest in the park's woodlands.

From the City Line Avenue entrance onto Interstate 76 East (Schuylkill Expressway), travel 0.6 miles along the ramp, then bear left onto U.S. 1 North (Roosevelt Blvd.) at the sign. Drive 20.5 miles on U.S. 1 North to I-95 North to Yardley (make sure to bear right at 17.3 miles for U.S. 1 North to Morrisville). Turn left at the light by the I-95 North sign. Travel 7 miles on I-95 North to the exit for New Hope and Yardley. Drive 0.3 miles on the offramp, then make a left toward New Hope at the stop sign. Follow the signs for Washington Crossing S.P. and Route 532 after making the left for 2.6 miles. Make a right onto Route 532 and drive 0.5 miles past the Washington Crossing S.P. entrance to Route 32 North. Turn left onto Route 32 North (River Road) and drive 4.2 miles to the sign for the Bowman's Hill Tower. Make a left onto Lurgan Road and drive 0.6 miles to the next sign for the tower. The tower is 0.6 miles up a steep grade to the right. After visiting the tower, return to Route 32 North, make a left, and continue for another 0.4 miles to the entrance for Bowman's Hill Wildflower Preserve on the left. Follow signs for another 0.3 miles along the park road to the headquarters off to the left. A one-way trip takes approximately one hour and fifteen minutes.

The most productive time is the first three weeks in May, as spring landbirds are funneling through on their northbound migration. Stop by the wildflower preserve headquarters for a detailed map of the area's nature trails. Four trails—Bucks County, Azalea, Bluebell, and Audubon—are especially good for migrants and are within easy reach of the headquarters. All are interconnected and can be comfortably walked in less than twenty minutes each. Various flycatchers, thrushes, vireos, and warblers pass through the adjoining woodlands in large numbers—similar to Ridley Creek. Look (listen!) for breeding Louisiana Waterthrush and Kentucky Warbler along the Audubon and Bluebell trails. Acadian Flycatcher used to breed regularly along Pidcock Creek (Bucks County and Azalea trails), but has recently been scarce. The Yellow-throated Vireo occasionally nests in the tall sycamores lining the creek.

Nearby Bowman's Hill Tower provides ready-made access to the woodland's treetops. This 110-foot tower affords a panoramic view of the Delaware River Valley and surrounding countryside. Migrating Tennessee and Blackburnian Warblers are easily observed as they pass through the uppermost stories of the ravine's deciduous hardwoods. Listen for the "wood-chippy" trill of the Worm-eating Warbler, which regularly nests along the drier slopes of the hill. In past years, the Cerulean Warbler bred here; however, Rick Mellon, the preserve's former naturalist, notes its absence in recent years.

Bull's Island is a narrow parcel of land sandwiched between the Delaware River and its adjoining canal on the New Jersey side of the river.

After leaving Bowman's Hill Wildflower Preserve, turn left back onto Route 32 North for 2.3 miles to the center of New Hope. Make a right across the bridge to Lambertville (travel 0.4 miles), then turn left onto Route 29 North. Drive 6.7 miles to the entrance for Bull's Island Camping Site (on Raven Rock). Make a left at the above sign, cross the canal bridge, and park by the headquarters.

Check the trees surrounding the headquarters for spring warblers and the breeding Chipping Sparrow. The Yellow-throated Warbler can often be found working the tall sycamore and cottonwood trees in the nearby camping grounds—especially around the shower stalls. The camping site is one hundred yards north of the headquarters along a gravel road. Also walk the trails south of the bridge across the canal (before reaching the headquarters). The Acadian

Flycatcher and Prothonotary Warbler regularly nest in this general area.

For more information, and the birdlist, write:

Bowman's Hill State Wildflower
    Preserve
Washington Crossing State Park
Washington Crossing, Pa. 18977
Phone: (215) 862-2924

Preserve headquarters is open daily 9:30 A.M.–5:00 P.M.

Pocono Mountains

"Pocono Mountains" refers to a vast expanse fanning from the Pocono escarpment in northeastern Pennsylvania eastward to the Delaware Water Gap–Stroudsburg, Pennsylvania, area. The dense coniferous forests around Pocono Lake, La Anna, and the more mountainous regions provide breeding habitat for Canadian Zone species not found southward. Approaching the mixed deciduous woodlands of the Delaware River Valley to the east, Alleghanian and then Carolinian avifauna predominate. Many birds, known only as migrants or winter residents in the Philadelphia area, breed in the varied habitats of the Poconos. Additionally, several boreal species (such as finches) winter in the region. Depending on the species, the birder must carefully select the proper location within the Poconos, as the area is composed of many diverse ecosystems.

The Pocono Mountains, with Stroudsburg as its conventional hub, is within a hundred mile, two and a half hour drive of Philadelphia. From the Valley Forge–King of Prussia entrance to the Pennsylvania Turnpike, bear right after the toll gate, following the signs for the Northeast Extension (New Jersey East and Allentown North). Drive east 7.5 miles along the turnpike and bear right at the exit for the Northeast Extension (Route 9). Travel 54.6 miles, and turn off at Exit 34 for Stroudsburg via Route 209. Drive 31.5 miles on Route 209 North to Marshall's Creek (Exit 52). The Delaware Water Gap Exit is 1 mile further on Route 209 North (Exit 53). Take the Marshall's Creek exit and continue 9.9 miles on Route 209 North (Interstate 80 East and Route 402 North are continuous with Route 209 for several miles) to the Delaware Water Gap National Recreational Area. Make a right at the sign; the headquarters is 0.8 miles further up the road.

Map 19
Bowman's Hill and Bull's Island

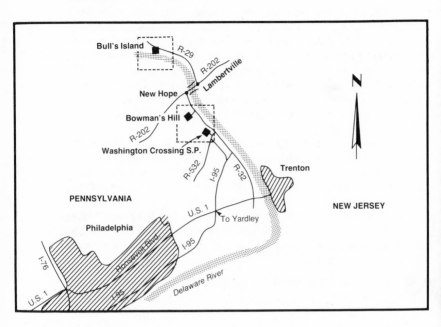

Map 20
Bull's Island

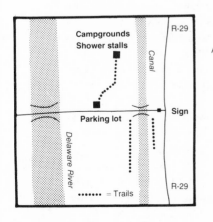

Map 21
Bowman's Hill

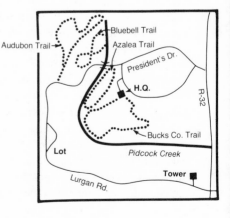

After leaving the Gap Recreational Area, turn right back onto Route 209 North. Drive 1.7 miles to the blinking light in Bushkill (Bushkill Falls is 2 miles to the left). Proceed past the blinking light on Route 209 North for 6.7 miles to the entrance for the Pocono Environmental Educational Center (PEEC). Make a left at the sign and wind up the steep grade for 0.9 miles to the headquarters. Stop off at the headquarters (open weekends) and pick up the regional bird list and map of the area trails.

After leaving the PEEC, turn right back onto Route 209 South. Travel 7.5 miles and turn hard left, continuing on Route 209 South (avoid going straight on Route 209 Business). Drive 3.6 miles further on Route 209 South and then bear left for Route 80 to the Delaware Water Gap. Travel another 1 mile to Exit 53 for Route 611 South to the Gap. The Delaware Water Gap overlook is 1.4 miles further along Route 611 South. The Appalachian Trail crosses Route 611 South one hundred yards before the overlook.

The general habitat of the Delaware Water Gap Recreational Area, PEEC, and the Delaware Water Gap itself is composed of mixed deciduous woodlands interrupted periodically by large coniferous stands. Alleghanian and Carolinian species predominate here, while a few Canadian Zone types breed in isolated pockets.

Other excellent birding spots, including Pocono Lake, La Anna, Hickory Run State Park, Beltzville Lake State Park, Long Pond, and Lake Wallenpaupack, are within easy reach of Stroudsburg. These areas are characterized by higher elevations and remnants of the "primeval forest"—islands of spruce, fir, and tamarack bogs that have escaped fire and the lumberman's axe. Canadian Zone species nest here. To reach these locations take Route 191 North, Route 80 West, or Route 209 South from the Stroudsburg area. Consult regional maps for exact directions.

As mentioned before, many birds nest in the Poconos that are not reliable summer residents elsewhere in the tri-state region. The best time to visit is during the breeding season—late May through early July—when the birds are likely to be in song. The following species regularly nest in the Poconos, although some are present in very small numbers: Sharp-shinned, Red-shouldered, and Broad-winged Hawks, Saw-whet Owl, Pileated Woodpecker, Alder Flycatcher, Least Flycatcher, Cliff Swallow, Red-breasted Nuthatch, Brown Creeper, Hermit Thrush, Golden-crowned King-

Map 22
Pocono Mountains

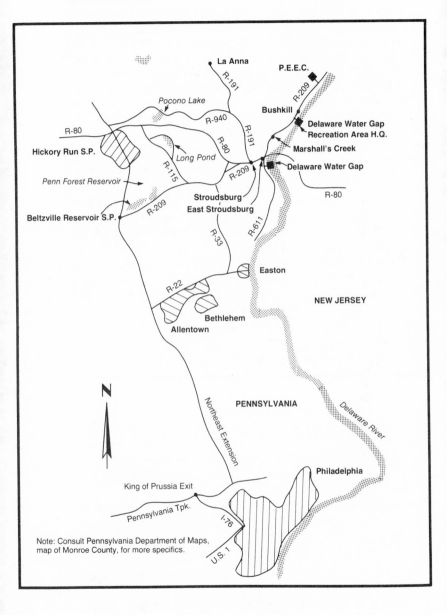

La Anna

P.E.E.C.

R-191

Pocono Lake

R-209

Bushkill

R-940

Delaware Water Gap
Recreation Area H.Q.

R-80

R-191

R-80

Marshall's Creek

Hickory Run S.P.

Long Pond

R-115

R-209

Delaware Water Gap

Penn Forest Reservoir

R-209

Stroudsburg
East Stroudsburg

R-80

Beltzville Reservoir S.P.

R-33

R-611

Easton

N

R-22

NEW JERSEY

Bethlehem

Allentown

PENNSYLVANIA

Northeast Extension

Delaware River

Philadelphia

King of Prussia Exit

Pennsylvania Tpk.

I-76

Note: Consult Pennsylvania Department of Maps,
map of Monroe County, for more specifics.

U.S. 1

let, Cedar Waxwing, Solitary Vireo, Black-and-white, Worm-eating, Golden-winged, Nashville, Magnolia, Black-throated Blue, Black-throated Green, Yellow-rumped (Myrtle), and Blackburnian Warblers, Northern and Louisiana Waterthrushes, Canada Warbler, Scarlet Tanager, Rose-breasted Grosbeak, Purple Finch, Dark-eyed (Slate-colored) Junco, and White-throated Sparrow. Northern Goshawk, Yellow-bellied Sapsucker, Olive-sided Flycatcher (probably), Winter Wren, Ruby-crowned Kinglet, Northern Parula and Pine Warblers, Pine Siskin, and Vesper Sparrow have nested occasionally. Yellow-bellied Flycatcher, Swainson's (Olive-backed) Thrush, and Mourning Warbler are former breeders that have disappeared in recent years.

The relative abundance of each species depends on the local habitat. For example, Street and Pettingill consider the Magnolia, Black-throated Green, and Blackburnian Warblers to be the commonest warblers in the coniferous forests surrounding the Pocono Lake region. These same birds are listed as uncommon or rare at the Pocono Environmental Educational Center (PEEC) near Stroudsburg. The Golden-winged, Blue-winged, Yellow, Chestnut-sided, and Prairie Warblers favor the more open, scrubby areas characteristic of the PEEC, which borders the Delaware River Valley.

Winter finches are another specialty of the Poconos. Evening Grosbeak, Purple Finch, Pine Grosbeak, Common Redpoll, Pine Siskin, and Red and White-winged Crossbills can often be found in evergreen stands throughout the colder months—especially during invasion years.

Consult Phillips Street's "Birds of the Pocono Mountains" for specific details on all the birds likely to be seen in the region.

For more information write:

Delaware Water Gap National
   Recreational Area
Bushkill, Pa. 18324
Phone: (717) 588-6637

Pocono Environmental
   Educational Center
R.D. I
Box 268
Dingmans Ferry, Pa. 18328
(Headquarters open on weekends)

Additional Pennsylvania Hot Spots

Audubon Wildlife Sanctuary   Audubon, Pa., near Valley Forge

State Park. Woodland birding similar to Ridley Creek. Phone: (215) 666-5593.

Churchville Reservoir (Springfield Lake Reservoir) Off Route 532 near Holland, Pa. Wintering waterfowl and breeding landbirds. Most famous for wintering Long-eared and Barn Owls in evergreen stands near headquarters. Phone: (215) 357-4005.

Four Mills Nature Reserve Ambler, Pa. Woodland birding. Phone: (215) 656-0267.

French Creek State Park Near Elverson, Pa. Woodland birding, including Broad-winged Hawk, Ruffed Grouse, and Pileated Woodpecker as summer residents. Phone: (215) 582-8125.

Green Lane Reservoir Off Route 29 near Green Lane, Pa. Wintering waterfowl.

Hay Creek Off Route 82 near Birdsboro, southeast of Reading, Pa. Woodland birding. Nesting species include: Acadian and Least Flycatchers, Yellow-throated Vireo, and Worm-eating, Northern Parula, Cerulean, Yellow-throated, and Hooded Warblers.

Lake Ontelaunee Near Maiden Creek north of Reading, Pa. Wintering waterfowl and migrating shorebirds. Active breeding colony of Cliff Swallows.

Longwood Gardens Near U.S. 1 at Kennett Square, Pa. Similar to Ridley Creek and Tyler Arboretum. Winter finches and nesting Eastern Bluebirds. Phone: (215) 388-6741.

Marsh Creek State Park Near the village of Eagle, outside of Downingtown, Pa. Wintering waterfowl. Phone: (215) 458-8515.

Middle Creek Wildlife Management Area Near Kleinfeltersville, north of Lancaster, Pa. Wintering waterfowl and breeding landbirds. Wintering Rough-legged Hawk and Northern Harrier (Marsh Hawk), nesting Ruffed Grouse and American Woodcock.

Penn Manor Off Route 13 near Tullytown, Pa. Wintering waterfowl and gulls, including Glaucous, Iceland, and Lesser Black-backed Gulls.

Pennypack Park Northeast Philadelphia. Woodland birding. Also a few open-area types, including Northern (Baltimore) and Orchard Orioles and Grasshopper Sparrow (formerly). Phone: (215) 671-0440.

Schuylkill Valley Nature Center   Hagy's Mill Road, Philadelphia. Woodland birding. Phone: (215) 482-7300.

New Jersey

Barnegat Lighthouse State Park (Long Beach Island) and Manahawkin National Wildlife Refuge

Long Beach Island, a narrow barrier beach, extends eighteen miles along coastal southcentral New Jersey. Barnegat Lighthouse State Park, at the extreme northern tip of the island, is a hot spot for wintering waterfowl. This area combines coastal inlets, sandy beaches, and rock jetties on the ocean side, with vast salt marshes on the Waterway side that separates the island from the nearby mainland.

To reach Barnegat Lighthouse from Philadelphia, proceed from the intersection of U.S. 1 (City Line Avenue) and the Schuylkill Expressway (I-76 East). Enter the Schuylkill Expressway (I-76 East) and drive 0.6 miles along the ramp, then bear left onto U.S. 1 North (Roosevelt Blvd.). Drive 7.2 miles on Roosevelt Blvd. (U.S. 1 North) to Robbins Avenue, following the signs for the Tacony-Palmyra Bridge. Make a right onto Robbins Avenue (Route 13 North) and travel 1.6 miles, then bear left for the bridge. Cross the bridge and pay 10¢ (1979) toll (1 mile further). This is now Route 73 East. Drive 9.9 miles on Route 73 East until reaching a circle. Go three-quarters way around the circle and follow the signs for Lakehurst and Route 70 East. Travel 17.7 miles on Route 70 East, passing two circles (at 5.5 and 10 miles). At the third circle, follow the signs for Long Beach Island and Route 72 East (one-quarter way around the circle). Drive 28 miles on Route 72 East to Long Beach Blvd. in town after crossing the bridge from the mainland (disregard the sign for Barnegat at the 15.8-mile mark and continue on Route 72 East to Long Beach Island). Long Beach Blvd. is 2.3 miles (the third traffic light) past the beginning of the bridge. Turn left onto Long Beach Blvd., following the signs for Surf City and Barnegat Lighthouse. Drive 8.2 miles along Long Beach Blvd., passing the towns of Harvey Cedars and Loveladies, to 8th Avenue (almost at the end of the island). Make a right and drive another 0.2 miles to a small parking lot by the dunes. Walk twenty yards up

through the dunes until you see the 8th Avenue jetty a little off to the right. You can reach the lighthouse by walking several hundred yards along the beach to the left. The lighthouse can also be reached by driving 0.4 miles further on Long Beach Blvd. past the intersection with 8th Avenue. Make a right at the stop sign, and the entrance to Barnegat Lighthouse State Park is 0.1 miles further. Park your car in the lot provided and walk forty yards to the bluff overlooking the bay and jetties. A one-way trip from Philadelphia to Barnegat Lighthouse takes approximately two hours.

The best time to visit Barnegat Lighthouse is during the colder months (November through early April). Large numbers of various seabirds can be observed from several vantage points, including the Lighthouse Inlet and the nearby 8th Avenue jetty. The jetty extends over a hundred yards into the Atlantic Ocean and is located less than one-half mile south of the lighthouse along the beach. During high tide the rocks are barely visible under the pounding surf, so time your visit for when the tide is out and the jetty is clearly seen. Horned Grebe, American Black Duck, Greater Scaup, Common Goldeneye, Bufflehead, Oldsquaw, all three Scoters, Ruddy Duck, and Red-breasted Merganser are common in the wash off the jetty. Redhead, Ring-necked Duck, Canvasback, Lesser Scaup, and Common Merganser are occasionally seen. Practically every winter, Red-necked Grebe, Common and King Eiders, and Harlequin Duck are reported here. Common and Red-throated Loons are frequently seen in the ocean beyond the jetty. Scope the nearby buoys for both Great (European) and Double-crested Cormorants during the colder months. Barnegat Lighthouse is the most reliable spot in the region to find the Great Cormorant. Scan the horizon for diving Northern Gannets, which are frequently observed from shore—especially during early November and April. During low tide, Purple Sandpipers work the jetty itself and the nearby winter beaches host pale Sanderlings.

The nearby Lighthouse Inlet is patrolled by various wintering gulls. Greater Black-backed, Herring, Ring-billed, and Bonaparte's Gulls are common. Check the April flocks of Bonaparte's for the Black-headed Gull, which is reported annually. Glaucous and Iceland Gulls and Black-legged Kittiwake are occasionally seen, and Lesser Black-backed and Little Gulls have also been recorded, although infrequently.

Search the ocean dunes and scrubby trees bordering the light-house parking lot for wintering sparrows—including the Ipswich race of the Savannah, Horned Lark, Snow Bunting, and an occa-sional Lapland Longspur. Migrating passerines stop off here dur-ing their spring and fall movements. Red and White-winged Cross-bills have been reported nearby, usually in small pine groves in residential areas.

The vast salt marshes on the Waterway side of Long Beach Is-land host large concentrations of wintering Brant. Rough-legged Hawk, Northern Harrier (Marsh Hawk), and Short-eared Owl can also be seen. Willet, herons, egrets, rails, and both Sharp-tailed and Seaside Sparrows round out the summer complement in these cordgrass meadows. The tidal flats attract various members of the plover and sandpiper family during their migrations.

Nearby Manahawkin National Wildlife Refuge is very similar to Brigantine in both habitats and representative species.

To reach Manahawkin N.W.R. from Long Beach Island, drive back 5.2 miles on Route 72 West to the Route 9 North cutoff. Bear right and drive 0.2 miles on the offramp to the stop sign at Route 9. Turn right onto Route 9 North and travel 0.1 miles to Stafford Avenue (immediately past the first light). Turn right onto Stafford Avenue by the firehouse and continue 1.4 miles until it turns into a dirt road. Stay on this road past woods and swamps until the little wooden bridge at the end of the marsh.

In addition to large numbers of ducks, herons, egrets, rails, and shorebirds, Manahawkin is one of the few regional hot spots where breeding Mute Swans are found. The extensive salt marshes provide suitable nesting sights for both Sharp-tailed and Seaside Sparrows. A hack was recently built in an effort to reestablish the Peregrine Falcon as an indigenous species—albeit using cap-tivity-raised birds. Whip-poor-wills call incessantly from the pine stands bordering the refuge. One should listen for the Chuck-will's-widow, which has invaded the area in very small numbers over the past few years. The main reason to visit Manahawkin is to glimpse the Black Rail during the breeding season (late May through early July). Search the cordgrass meadows at the end of the dirt road through the refuge for this elusive species. To increase your chances of seeing (hearing) this rare bird, listen for its distinctive call between dusk and dawn.

For more information, write to Brigantine National Wildlife Refuge, which administers Manahawkin N.W.R.

Holgate Peninsula, Long Beach Island

The Holgate Unit of Brigantine N.W.R. is located on the extreme southern tip of Long Beach Island, forty-one car miles northeast of the Brigantine headquarters. This 256-acre refuge, consisting of barrier beach, sand dunes, and mud flats, provides ideal habitat for migrating shorebirds and breeding terns, rails, shorebirds, and sparrows. During the nesting season the dunes are off-limits, so birders must walk three miles along the beach to reach the mudflats on the other side of the island. A walk along the surf and adjoining dunes offers an excellent chance to view several oceanside birds not common elsewhere in the region due to shrinking habitat. A trek to the mudflats on the other side of the peninsula is recommended only if you are in good shape and if the weather is mild. The migrating and nesting shorebirds using these mudflats are also seen nearby Tuckerton Meadows, to which they regularly commute from Holgate. Tuckerton is readily accessible by car.

Proceed as before to Barnegat Lighthouse State Park. Turn off Route 70 East at the circle onto Route 72 East (following the signs for Long Beach Island). Drive 25.7 miles to the beginning of the bridge to Long Beach Island. Travel another 2.2 miles across the bridge to the third light (Bay Avenue). Make a right onto Bay Avenue and drive 9.1 miles to the dead-end parking lot by the Holgate Unit. One must walk approximately three miles along the beach to reach the mudflats on the other side of the peninsula as the dunes are closed. A one-way trip from Philadelphia to Holgate takes just under two hours.

The best times to visit Holgate are during the spring migration (May), summer breeding season, and fall migration (August through September). Walking along the beach in early May, check the ocean for late-moving seafowl. Various ducks, Common and Red-throated Loons in nuptial plumage, and tardy Northern Gannets have been seen. Sanderlings are common along the beach, while several pairs of breeding Piping Plover can be found among the dunes. Holgate is one of the most reliable locations in the region to observe this dwindling species. Wilson's Plover used to nest in the area and should be looked for if it stages a local comeback. Roseate Tern is in the same category. Happily, a breeding pair of Roseates were present in 1978. Common and Little (Least) Terns and Black Skimmer are usually seen patrolling the surf, and small breeding colonies may still exist among the dunes. During the fall migration (late August through September), large numbers of Royal Terns concentrate at Holgate. A few Caspian Terns are also present. The accidental Sandwich Tern has also been recorded as recently as 1978. Seaside Sparrow and an occasional Horned Lark and Savannah Sparrow use the scrubby vegetated dunes for nesting. The Ipswich race of the Savannah Sparrow can be found here during the winter months. The birds frequenting the mudflats on the Waterway side of the peninsula are covered in the Tuckerton Meadows section.

For more information, write to Brigantine National Wildlife Refuge, which administers the Holgate Unit.

Tuckerton Meadows, Tuckerton

Tuckerton Meadows, between Little Egg Harbor and Great Bay on the southcentral coast of New Jersey, consists of vast salt marshes, brackish pools, and tidal mudflats. Migrating and nesting shorebirds commute between here and the adjacent Holgate peninsula during the warmer months.

To reach Tuckerton Meadows, drive back from Holgate to the center of the town of Ship Bottom. Make a left at the light onto Route 72 West and travel 5.4 miles on Route 72 West to Route 9 South. Bear right, following the signs for Atlantic City, and loop around the cloverleaf onto Route 9 South (0.15 miles separate the Route 9 North and Route 9 South Exits). Drive 7.7 miles on Route 9 South to Route 539 at the light in the center of Tuckerton. Drive another 0.2 miles on Route 9 South past Route 539 (passing a lake on the right) to a left turnoff. Make a left at the sign for Great Bay Blvd. and proceed 6.6 miles to the earthen parking lot by the bay. This narrow road crosses several one-lane wooden bridges along the way.

Salt marshes, inland waterways, and tidal pools line the six-mile gravel road from Tuckerton to the birding area at the end of the peninsula. Great Blue and Little Blue Herons, Great (Common) and Snowy Egrets, Black-crowned Night and Louisiana Herons, Glossy Ibis, Clapper Rail, and Willet are common during the summer. Least and American Bitterns and Yellow-crowned Night Heron are occasionally seen. Black Rail is also present during the breeding season but is more likely heard than seen (listen between dusk and dawn). Sora and Virginia Rail can be found here during their migrations. Check the scattered nesting platforms along the way for Ospreys, which breed here every year. Red-winged Blackbird and Sharp-tailed and Seaside Sparrows nest in the cordgrass meadows, while Yellow Warbler, Common Yellow-throat, and Song Sparrow favor the scrubby thickets lining the road.

At the end of the road, near the entrance to the Rutgers University Experimental Station, tidal mudflats attract large numbers of migrating shorebirds in May and again from August through September. American Oystercatcher (nests here), Semipalmated and Black-bellied Plovers, Ruddy Turnstone, Whimbrel, Greater and Lesser Yellowlegs, Red Knot, Pectoral Sandpiper (fall), Least and Semipalmated Sandpipers, Dunlin, Short-billed Dowitcher, Western Sandpiper (fall), and Sanderling are common during low tide. Lesser (American) Golden Plover, Long-billed Dowitcher (late fall), Marbled and Hudsonian Godwits, Stilt Sandpiper, and Northern and Wilson's Phalaropes are occasionally seen, especially in late summer (mid-August through September). Curlew Sandpiper and Ruff are reported annually (mid- to late May), as are other rarities.

During the winter months, Northern Harrier (Marsh Hawk) and an occasional Rough-legged Hawk and Short-eared Owl can be seen patrolling the desolate marshes. Be on the lookout for Snowy Owl and Northern Shrike, which occasionally stray into the area during their invasion years. Large flocks of Brant gather in the sheltered inlets of Great Bay and Little Egg Harbor, as do various sea ducks.

Mercer Sod Farm, Columbus

Mercer Sod Farm is located in Burlington County, New Jersey, just south of the town of Columbus. This large turf farm is little more than a stone's throw from Philadelphia across the Tacony-Palmyra Bridge. Mowed grass plots alternate with dirt tracts where the sod was recently harvested. The surrounding countryside is

Map 23
Barnegat Lighthouse State Park, Long Beach Island, New Jersey

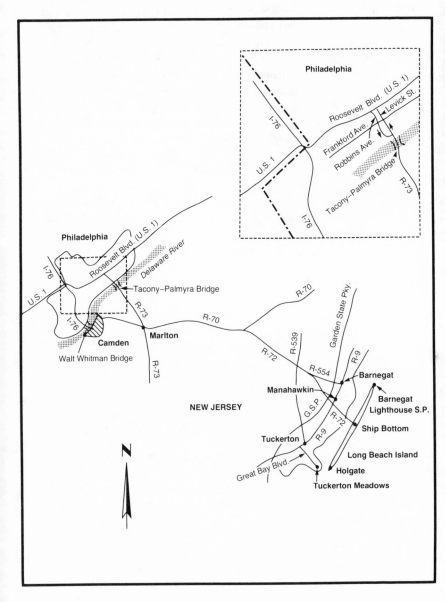

Map 24
Long Beach Island Area: Barnegat Lighthouse S.P., Manahawkin N.W.R.,
Holgate, and Tuckerton

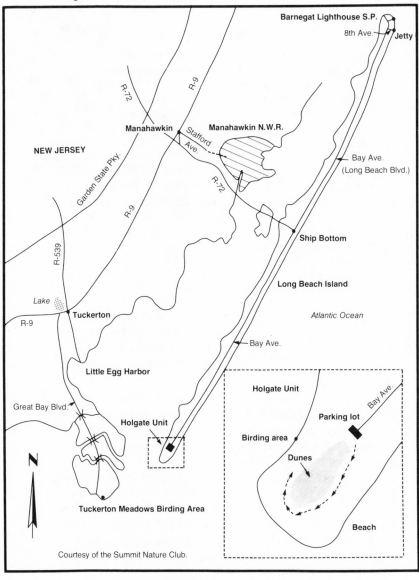

Courtesy of the Summit Nature Club.

dotted with other turf farms, cultivated fields, and scrubby pastures. During fall migration, this area draws various upland meadow and tundra species that are not regularly seen elsewhere in the region.

To reach the Mercer Sod Farm proceed as before to the Tacony-Palmyra Bridge (see directions to Barnegat Lighthouse). After the toll (10¢ in 1979) continue on Route 73 East for 5.4 miles. Make a right at the turnoff for Route 38 East to Mount Holly (this exit is 0.1 miles past the Route 38 West turnoff). Drive 13.4 miles on Route 38 East to a busy intersection, then make a left onto Route 206 North. Continue on Route 206 North for 4.7 miles to the junction with Spur Route 528. The Mercer Sod Farm is on your left, stretching for approximately one mile before this intersection (roughly 1.4 miles past Route 537). A one-way trip from the City Line Avenue entrance onto the Schuylkill Expressway takes approximately one hour and fifteen minutes. Park your car well off the shoulder of Route 206. Carefully walk across this busy thoroughfare and birdwatch from the side of the road. "Keep off the grass," so you do not ruin this hot spot for other birders.

The best time to visit Mercer Sod Farm is from late August through mid-September. Labor Day weekend is ideal. A good zoom scope is essential. Set up on the grassy knoll near the junction of Route 206 North and Spur Route 528, or walk the shoulder along Route 206, stopping periodically to glass the fields—but be careful of cars. Killdeer, Lesser (American) Golden and Black-bellied Plovers, Upland Sandpiper (Plover), Pectoral and Buff-breasted Sandpipers, various "peep," and Eastern Meadowlark are common. The Solitary Sandpiper is occasionally seen. This is the best location in the tri-state region to observe the Lesser Golden Plover, Upland Sandpiper, and Buff-breasted Sandpiper. The Upland Sandpiper, in flocks of up to twenty birds at a time, favors the grassy fields. The Lesser Golden Plover and Buff-breasted Sandpiper are equally at home on the denuded flats or the expansive green turf. Upwards of thirty Lesser Golden Plovers have been seen at one time, while the Buff-breasted Sandpiper is usually observed in twos or threes.

Flocks of Horned Lark and an occasional Bobolink are also encountered in the area during this period. Search the barren fields

Map 25
Mercer Sod Farm

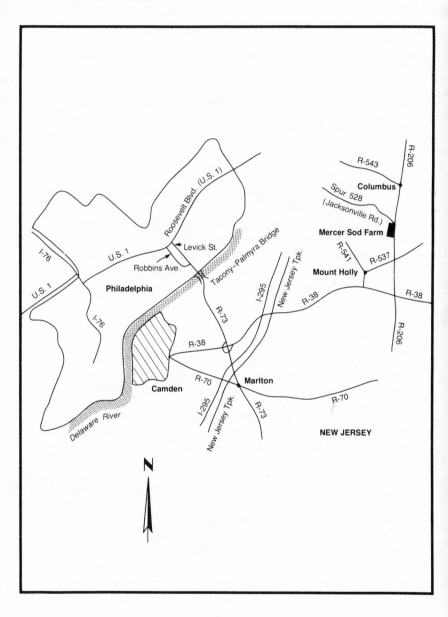

later in the season—late October through the winter—for Horned
Lark, Water Pipit, Snow Bunting, and stray Lapland Longspurs.

For more information and last-minute birding updates, call or
write:

Rancocas Nature Center
c/o Liz Anderson
R.D. 1
Rancocas Road
Mount Holly, N.J. 08060
Phone: (609) 261-2495

Princeton, Mercer County

Princeton, located in Mercer County in central New Jersey, is
one of the most productive birding areas in the tri-state region.
The fifty-acre Princeton Wildlife Refuge, the adjacent five-hun-
dred–acre forest behind the Institute for Advanced Studies, and
the nearby Wargo Road Watershed are all famous for the large
number and variety of birds seen year-round, especially during
spring migration. These locales offer a rich panorama of habitats.
Fresh-water marsh in the wildlife refuge, deciduous woodlands in
the Institute Woods, and open scrubby fields in the watershed area
attract hordes of migrating landbirds and several nesting "specialties."

**To reach Princeton, drive 27.8 miles on U.S. 1 North from
the City Line Avenue entrance onto the Schuylkill Expressway.
Pay the toll (15¢ in 1979) at the bridge crossing the Delaware
River into Trenton. Travel 11.2 miles on U.S. 1 North (Tren-
ton Freeway) to Route 571 West and Princeton. Bear right at
the exit and loop around the cloverleaf to the left for Route
571 West. Drive 1.6 miles along Route 571 West to Nassau
Street. Turn left at the light onto Nassau and drive 0.35 miles
to Mercer Street, which is the left turn immediately before the
Route 206 South turnoff. After making the left onto Mercer
Street, travel 0.7 miles to Olden Lane. Turn left onto Olden
Lane and drive another 0.6 miles to the parking lot by the
Institute Woods. A one-way trip from City Line Avenue to
Princeton takes approximately one hour and thirty minutes.**

The best times to visit Princeton are during the spring migration
(first three weeks in May) and the summer breeding season. After
parking in the lot at the end of Olden Lane, walk the well-marked

trail immediately behind the Institute for Advanced Studies. At least thirty-five species of warblers have been recorded in the general area in early to mid-May. Black-and-white, Blue-winged, Northern Parula, Yellow, Magnolia, Black-throated Blue, Black-throated Green, Yellow-rumped (Myrtle), Blackburnian, Chestnut-sided, Bay-breasted, Blackpoll, and Palm Warblers, Ovenbird, Northern and Louisiana Waterthrushes, Kentucky Warbler, Common Yellowthroat, Canada Warbler, and American Redstart are common. Worm-eating, Golden-winged, Tennessee, Nashville, Cape May, Pine, Prairie, and Wilson's Warblers are less frequently seen. Several hundred yards up the trail, turn left at the stone and bronze plaque and continue downhill toward Stony Brook Bridge. After about a hundred yards, Pipeline Path crosses the main trail. The Kentucky Warbler regularly nests along this path between here and the now-distant parking lot. Wood, Swainson's (Olive-backed), and Gray-cheeked Thrushes and Veery are common during spring migration. Northern (Baltimore) Oriole, Scarlet Tanager, and Rose-breasted Grosbeak also pass through the area in large numbers and may remain to breed. Continue downhill toward Stony Brook Creek. Check the marsh to the left of the bridge for Red-winged Blackbird, Yellow Warbler, Common Yellowthroat, and Swamp Sparrow, among others. Search the tall deciduous trees lining the creek for nesting Red-eyed, Warbling, and Yellow-throated Vireos.

After the bridge, continue downstream along Stony Brook Trail until it runs into the marsh by the pumping station. The Prothonotary Warbler regularly breeds in the swampy woodlands adjoining this trail. The Connecticut Warbler is frequently seen in the scrubby thickets lining the paths around the marsh from mid-September through mid-October. The Orange-crowned Warbler has also been recorded here during fall migration.

The marsh and pumping station (part of the Princeton Wildlife Refuge) can also be reached by car. From the Olden Lane parking lot drive 0.15 miles along Hardin Road. At the stop sign make a hard right and proceed along the dirt road past the observation tower to the pumping station. The observation tower overlooks the marsh and provides a chance to glimpse the resident herons, bitterns, and rails. Nesting Wood Ducks are also seen.

The Wargo Road Watershed area is a much different environment. Plowed fields, overgrown meadows, and scrubby thickets attract a discriminating clientele unlike that of the Institute Woods and the Princeton Wildlife Refuge.

From the Institute Woods parking lot, drive back on Olden Lane to Mercer Street. Make a left onto Mercer Street and travel 2.3 miles to Province Line Road. Turn right onto Province Line Road and proceed another 2.3 miles to Rosedale Road (second stop sign). Make a left onto Rosedale Road and drive 0.9 miles to Carter Road (three-way intersection). Turn right onto Carter Road and travel 0.7 miles to a left turnoff at Bayberry Road (second street to the left). Drive 1.5 miles on Bayberry Road (dirt road in part) and make a right onto Pennington–Rocky Hill Road. Proceed 0.6 miles on that road and then make a left onto Moore's Mill–Mt. Rose Road. Drive approximately 0.4 miles on Mt. Rose Road to the third left, which is Wargo Road. Make a left and continue 0.6 miles up Wargo Road to an old barn off to the right.

The fields along the dirt road past the barn (continuation of Wargo Road) attract nesting Bobolink and Grasshopper Sparrow, plus an occasional Vesper Sparrow. Henslow's Sparrow has also, but rarely, been recorded here. Check the fields during the winter months for Horned Lark, Water Pipit, Snow Bunting, and an occasional Lapland Longspur. Along Moore's Mill–Mt. Rose Road (past the Wargo Road entrance) overgrown pastures studded with thickets and isolated groves of trees host breeding Blue-winged and Prairie Warblers, Yellow-breasted Chat, and Orchard Oriole. When driving to Wargo Road from Princeton, scan the sod farms along Province Line Road for fall plovers and sandpipers (see the Mercer Sod Farm section). Also stop off at the Educational Testing Service on Carter Road for nesting Eastern Bluebirds, which favor the wooden boxes erected along the power lines and open fields.

Winter birding can also be rewarding at Princeton. The annual Christmas Count tallies close to one hundred species. Cooper's and Red-shouldered Hawks, Barn, Common Screech, Great Horned, and Long-eared Owls, Winter Wren, Pine Siskin, White-crowned Sparrow, and Snow Bunting are among the regulars. The Princeton count provides one of the best chances in the region of seeing the Saw-whet Owl and Northern Shrike. Search the fairly

Map 26
Princeton

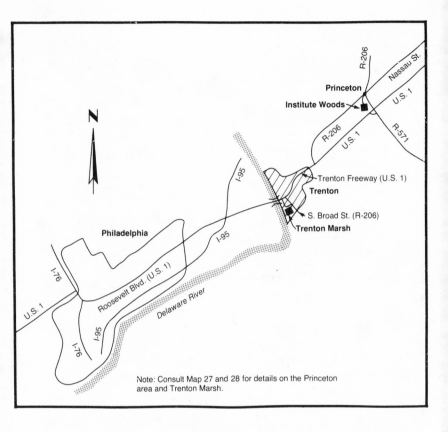

R-206

Nassau St.

Princeton

Institute Woods

U.S. 1

R-206

R-571

N

U.S. 1

I-95

Trenton Freeway (U.S. 1)

Trenton

Philadelphia

I-95

S. Broad St. (R-206)

Trenton Marsh

I-76

Roosevelt Blvd. (U.S. 1)

U.S. 1

I-95

I-76

Delaware River

Note: Consult Map 27 and 28 for details on the Princeton area and Trenton Marsh.

Map 27
The Princeton Area

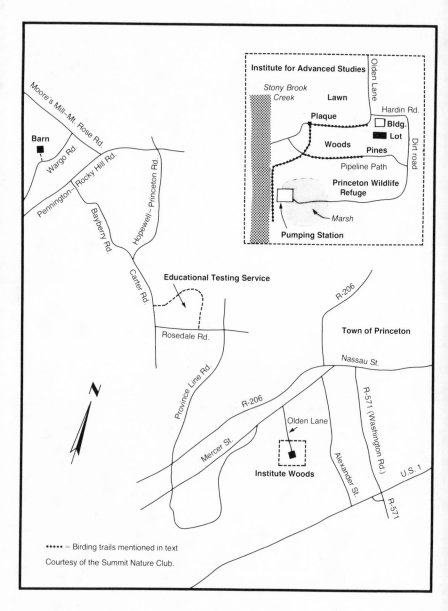

Institute for Advanced Studies

Olden Lane

Stony Brook
Creek

Lawn

Hardin Rd.

Plaque

Bldg.

Woods

Lot

Pines

Dirt road

Pipeline Path

Princeton Wildlife
Refuge

Marsh

Pumping Station

Barn

Moore's Mill–Mt. Rose Rd.

Wargo Rd.

Rocky Hill Rd.

Pennington–Rocky Hill Rd.

Hopewell–Princeton Rd.

Bayberry Rd.

Carter Rd.

Educational Testing Service

R-206

Town of Princeton

Rosedale Rd.

Nassau St.

Province Line Rd.

R-206

R-571 (Washington Rd.)

Olden Lane

Mercer St.

Institute Woods

Alexander St.

U.S. 1

R-571

••••• = Birding trails mentioned in text

Courtesy of the Summit Nature Club.

extensive pine woods below the Olden Lane parking lot for Long-eared Owls, nuthatches, and winter finches.

Trenton Marsh, Trenton

Trenton Marsh, within the John A. Roebling Memorial Park, is a three-hundred-acre refuge straddling the Delaware River just south of Trenton, New Jersey. Fresh-water swamps, shallow ponds, and woodlands attract a large variety of species; the preserve is especially good for marsh birding. Similar to Tinicum in both habitat and birdlife, Trenton Marsh has the advantage of more extensive wooded areas. But for waterfowl, Trenton Marsh cannot compete with Tinicum's larger impoundment.

To reach Trenton Marsh from Philadelphia, proceed as before to the toll bridge (15¢ in 1979) crossing the Delaware River into Trenton. After the toll continue on U.S. 1 North (Trenton Expressway) and take the first exit, which is 0.3 miles further. Bear right for the exit, following the signs for Route 29. Continue on the offramp past several intersections for 0.2 miles to the junction with the John Fitch Parkway. Make a left onto the Parkway, which soon runs into Lamberton Street. Bear right onto Lamberton and drive 0.75 miles to Lalor Street (total of 1 mile from ramp exit to Lalor Street). Make a left onto Lalor Street following the signs for Route 206 South. Drive 1.1 miles on Lalor Street to South Broad Street. Make a right and travel 0.2 miles on South Broad Street past the Roman Catholic church to Sewell Avenue. Make a right onto Sewell Avenue (at the 1800 block) and drive past three intersections for 0.2 miles to a dead end. Turn left onto the dirt road and go down the hill for 0.1 miles to a large parking lot. Start birding here, or turn right onto the dike road. Drive another 0.2 miles along the dike to a smaller lot from which several trails radiate. A one-way trip to Trenton Marsh from Philadelphia takes a little over one hour.

The best times to visit Trenton Marsh are during spring migration (May) and the summer breeding season. Great Blue, Green, and Black-crowned Night Herons are frequently seen working the pond edges during the warmer months. King and Virginia Rails and Sora nest in the heavily vegetated marshes to the right of the parking lot. These secretive birds are difficult to glimpse but can often be heard calling just before dawn. Least and American Bitterns favor the swampy areas along the trail leading off to the left from the smaller parking lot at the end of the dike road. This trail winds through marsh and lowland woods and, after 150 yards, runs into a crossdike. Bear right here and continue to walk the trail. Check the stubby willows and bushes along this dike for breeding Willow ("Fitz-Bew") Flycatcher, Yellow Warbler, and Common Yellowthroat, which are all common. Pied-billed Grebe, Wood Duck, Common Gallinule, and Marsh (Long-billed Marsh) Wren round out the marshbirds likely to be seen.

Check the fairly extensive wooded areas surrounding the picnic grove in Roebling Park for spring landbird migrants. To reach Roebling Park drive straight ahead for 0.7 miles from the central parking lot. American Redstart, Northern (Baltimore) Oriole, and Rose-breasted Grosbeak, among others, stay the summer. After dark listen for the distinctive call of the Barred Owl, which regularly nests in the wetter portions of the adjoining woodlands. During the colder months, Trenton Marsh is as good a place as any to see the Common Snipe and Winter Wren.

Ocean City: Corson's Inlet and Ocean Crest State Park

In addition to being a famous summer resort, Ocean City, New Jersey, provides year-round birdwatching opportunities. Just outside the southern limits of Ocean City, Corson's Inlet and Ocean Crest State Park include several different salt-water and brackish habitats. A mixture of coastal inlets, salt marshes, barrier dunes, and the Atlantic surf itself attracts a large number and variety of birds, depending on the season.

To reach Ocean City, New Jersey, proceed from the junction of U.S. 1 (City Line Avenue) and the Schuylkill Expressway (Route 76 East). Follow the directions for Brigantine to the Egg Harbor Toll Plaza on the Atlantic City Expressway. After the toll ($1.00 in 1979) drive 9.9 miles to the Garden State Parkway South (Exit 7 South)—this is 2.2 miles past Exit 9 for Absecon and Brigantine. Bear right onto the Garden State Parkway South and travel 11.7 miles to Exit 25 for Ocean City and Marmora (this is the second exit for Ocean City). Take Exit 25 off to the right and drive 0.15 miles on the exit ramp to the stop sign. Make a left onto 34th Street and continue for 2 miles to Asbury Avenue (third light after the bridge). Make a right onto Asbury Avenue and travel 2.1 miles to 55th Street (next light), which is Ocean Drive. Make a right onto 55th Street

Map 28
Trenton Marsh: Roebling Memorial Park

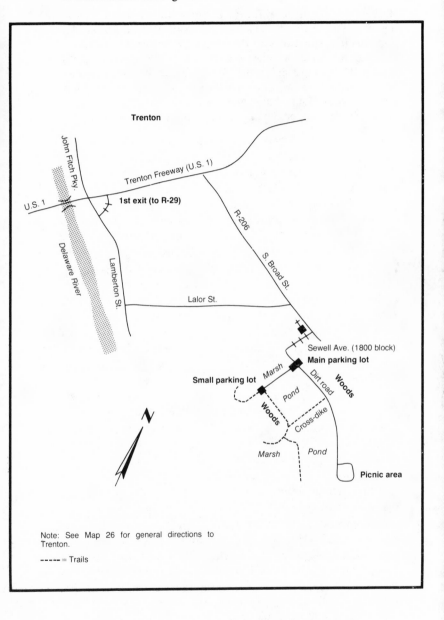

(Ocean Drive) and continue for 1 mile to the fishermen's parking lot at Ocean Crest. Park here and walk along the inlet edge
and through the dunes to the ocean. After birding this area
proceed to Corson's Inlet, which is 0.7 miles further along
Ocean Drive. Park off to the side of the busy road. Corson's
Inlet is to your left, while expansive salt marshes border Ocean
Drive to your right. Allow one hour and thirty minutes for a
one-way trip (longer during the crowded tourist season).

A visit to Ocean City during any season can be rewarding. The
colder months (November through April) afford birders a chance
to see typical wintering waterfowl native to the Atlantic Coast.
Scope the ocean surf off the dunes of Ocean Crest State Park for
both Common and Red-throated Loons, plus the ubiquitous Oldsquaw. All three species of Scoters pass by this vantage point, as
does the early spring Double-crested Cormorant movement. You
must walk several hundred yards of vegetated sand dunes on the
way to the beach from the parking lot. This is one of the best areas
in the region to observe the Ipswich race of the Savannah Sparrow
during the winter months—plus an assorted lot of sparrows,
Horned Larks, and an occasional Snow Bunting.

The fury of the Atlantic surf mellows as it rushes into the calmer
waters of Corson's Inlet. During the winter, Horned Grebe, American Black Duck, Greater Scaup, Common Goldeneye, Bufflehead,
Oldsquaw, Ruddy Duck, and Common and Red-breasted Mergansers are frequently seen. Brant, various puddle ducks, the rarely
observed Redhead, Ring-necked Duck, Canvasback, and American Coot are occasionally reported. In recent years, increasing
numbers of Boat-tailed Grackle have been tallied on the Christmas
Counts; a few pairs may remain to breed.

Spring ushers in a new lineup of species. From late April through
mid-May, herons, egrets, and an occasional Whimbrel visit the salt
marshes, while the inlet's tidal flats host numerous shorebird migrants. American Oystercatcher, Semipalmated and Black-bellied
Plovers, Ruddy Turnstone, Spotted Sandpiper, Willet, Greater
and Lesser Yellowlegs, Red Knot, Pectoral Sandpiper, assorted
"peep," Dunlin, Short-billed Dowitcher, and Sanderling are common now. A repeat performance occurs during the fall migration
(mid-August through mid-September).

The summer months (June through early August) cater to a different bird-fare. Herons and egrets, plus breeding Willet and Clap-

per Rail, are found in the adjoining salt marshes. The Sharp-tailed Sparrow hides in these meadows of ankle-high cordgrass. The Seaside Sparrow favors the taller grass lining the channels and the scrubby areas near the saline pool. Breeding Piping Plover use the saline pool located two hundred yards south of the entrance to Corson's Inlet along the ocean side of the road. This is one of the few reliable spots in the region where Piping Plover can still be found nesting. Continue south past this pool to the bridge crossing the inlet. Black Skimmer, Common Tern, and at least several pairs of American Oystercatcher work the sand bars exposed by the tide. Small congregations of Royal Tern gather here during their fall movement (late August through September). The brushy thickets lining Ocean Drive are frequented by migrating landbirds, especially warblers and sparrows.

Stone Harbor Bird Sanctuary and Avalon Causeway

Stone Harbor Bird Sanctuary is a famous heronry that was rescued at the last minute from the ever-encroaching resort building that has decimated the Jersey Coast. The 21-acre preserve is located at the southern end of Stone Harbor, New Jersey. Consisting of dense groves of medium-height trees and low scrub, it provides nesting sites for all the herons, egrets, and bitterns indigenous to the Delaware Valley region. The nearby salt marshes of Nummy Island serve both as feeding grounds for these birds and as a welcome oasis for migrating shorebirds. You can view most of the sanctuary's species from the central parking lot at 114th Street. A walk around the fenced-in perimeter is recommended for finding the more elusive Yellow-crowned Night Heron.

To reach Stone Harbor Sanctuary, proceed as before to Ocean City, New Jersey. Continue on the Garden State Parkway South for 15.1 miles past the Ocean City and Marmora exit. Turn left at Exit 10 for Stone Harbor (Route 29). Stop off at the Wetlands Institute (2.8 miles after turning left for Stone Harbor). An observation tower atop the headquarters overlooks the outlying salt marshes. After birding the institute, cross the Intracoastal Waterway and drive another 0.7 miles on Stone Harbor Blvd. to Ocean Drive. This is the third light in town; make a right. Travel 1 mile on Ocean Drive to the sanctuary parking lot at 114th Street. A one-way trip from Ocean City usually takes under one-half hour.

Map 29
Ocean City, New Jersey: Corson's Inlet and Ocean Crest State Park

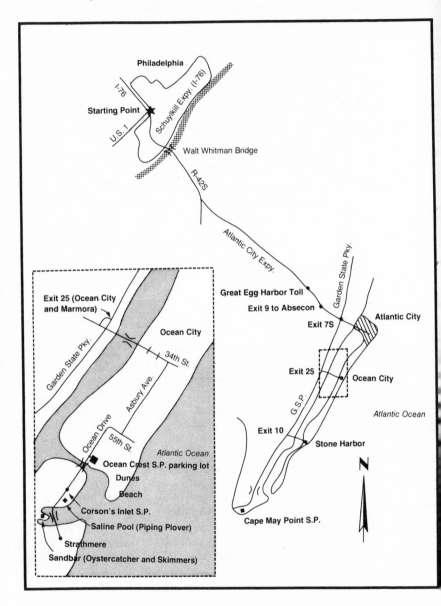

The sanctuary is busy from early spring (April) well into fall. By May most species have started nesting, while August and September are noted for large numbers of immature birds loafing at the preserve. Late summer is also the best time for such stragglers as the White Ibis, which is recorded almost yearly. Dawn and dusk, when the birds move to and from their feeding grounds, are the best times. Good concentrations of Great (Common) and Snowy Egrets, Black-crowned Night and Louisiana Herons, and Glossy Ibis can be found during the warmer months. Lesser numbers of Great Blue, Green, and Little Blue Herons and Cattle Egret are also seen. The several pairs of Yellow-crowned Night Herons that nest in the sanctuary are one of the main reasons to visit. Again, you must search carefully among the dense groves lining the refuge's borders to find this secretive bird.

Nummy Island is a vast salt marsh that connects Stone Harbor Sanctuary with the nearby Wildwood resorts. From Stone Harbor's parking lot, drive south 0.7 miles along Ocean Drive to the bridge for Nummy Island. Tidal pools, mudflats, and cordgrass meadows line the road for just over one mile leading to the toll bridge for the Wildwoods. Birds from the heronry and migrating shorebirds use this area. The salt marshes provide nesting habitat for Clapper Rail, Willet, and Sharp-tailed and Seaside Sparrows. Common, Forster's, and Little (Least) Terns and Black Skimmer are also seen.

After birding the sanctuary, you should visit the nearby Avalon Osprey Colony.

Once back on the Garden State Parkway, drive north 3.6 miles back toward Avalon. Take the exit for Avalon and travel 0.2 miles on the offramp to the stop sign. Make a left onto the Avalon Causeway (Route 1) and drive another 2.5 miles to the colony, which is off to the right.

This is the largest concentration of breeding Ospreys in the tri-state region. The platform nests among the stunted cedars are easily seen from the road. From mid-April through September, the colony is active with at least a half-dozen birds present at any one time. Nesting terns and Black Skimmer are also found.

For more information, write:

Stone Harbor Borough Hall
Stone Harbor, N.J. 08247

Wetlands Institute
Stone Harbor Blvd.
Stone Harbor, N.J. 08247
Phone: (609) 368-1211

Map 30
Stone Harbor Bird Sanctuary and Avalon Osprey Colony

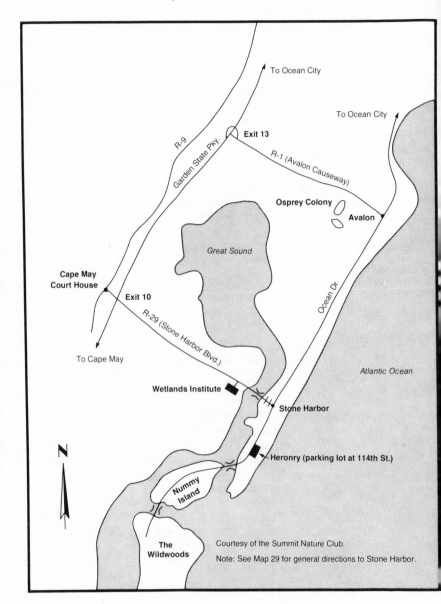

To Ocean City

To Ocean City

R-9

Garden State Pky.

Exit 13

R-1 (Avalon Causeway)

Osprey Colony

Avalon

Great Sound

Cape May
Court House

Exit 10

R-29 (Stone Harbor Blvd.)

Ocean Dr.

To Cape May

Atlantic Ocean

Wetlands Institute

Stone Harbor

N

Heronry (parking lot at 114th St.)

Nummy
Island

The
Wildwoods

Courtesy of the Summit Nature Club.

Note: See Map 29 for general directions to Stone Harbor.

Additional New Jersey Hot Spots

Assunpink Game Management Area   North of Allentown, N.J., in southwest Monmouth County. Loose breeding colony (at least several pairs) of Blue Grosbeaks.

Cape May Courthouse   Near Stone Harbor, N.J. Loose breeding colony (several pairs) of Red-headed Woodpeckers have traditionally nested at the County Park, approximately one mile from the Courthouse.

Dividing Creek   Cumberland County, N.J., south of Millville. Habitat similar to the mixed southern hardwood–pine forests characteristic of the Pocomoke River drainage of the Delmarva Peninsula. The following species have recently bred or are suspected of breeding: Black Rail, Chuck-will's-widow, Acadian Flycatcher, Sedge (Short-billed Marsh) Wren, Prothonotary, Worm-eating, Yellow-throated, and Northern Parula Warblers, and Summer Tanager.

Fortescue   Southern Cumberland County, N.J., south of Bridgeton. Breeding Willet, Boat-tailed Grackle, and marsh sparrows. Snow Goose, Northern Harrier (Marsh Hawk), and Short-eared Owl during the colder months.

Island Beach State Park   East of Toms River, N.J., along the northcentral coast. Habitat and birdlife similar to Long Beach Island (Barnegat Lighthouse State Park and Holgate Unit).

Killcohook National Wildlife Refuge   Northwest of Salem, N.J., along the Delaware River. Other spots in the general area include Supawna National Wildlife Refuge and Mannington Creek. Migrating waterfowl, especially puddle ducks and geese in the fall. Also, summer waders (herons, egrets, etc.) and winter birds of prey (Northern Harrier, Short-eared Owl, and an occasional eagle). Under the administration of Brigantine National Wildlife Refuge.

Parvin State Park   Southeastern Salem County, N.J., outside of Vineland. Breeding Summer Tanager, plus several others found in the Dividing Creek area. Phone: (609) 692-7039.

Pine Barrens   Burlington County in southcentral New Jersey. This vast wilderness includes several state forests and parks: Lebanon State Forest, Penn State Forest, Wharton State Forest, and

Batsto Village. Breeding Ruffed Grouse, Wood Duck, Saw-whet Owl, Whip-poor-will, an occasional Chuck-will's-widow, and Black-and-white, Prothonotary, Northern Parula, Pine, Prairie, and Hooded Warblers. Also good for winter finches, with Red Crossbills sometimes lingering well into April. Phone: (609) 726-1191 for Lebanon and (609) 561-0024 for Wharton Tract.

Shark River Inlet   South of Asbury Park, N.J. Wintering water-fowl and gulls. Famous for the Barrow's Goldeneye, which has wintered here for the past ten years.

Delaware

Brandywine Creek State Park and Wilmington Christmas Count

Brandywine Creek State Park is a 434-acre preserve that hugs the western side of Brandywine Creek as it meanders through northern Delaware. The habitats and birdlife are similar to those of the Ridley Creek–Tyler Arboretum area. Deciduous woodlands, rolling meadows, scrubby thickets, and the Brandywine floodplain provide year-round birdwatching opportunities. Landbirds and some fresh-water marsh species are the main attraction.

To reach Brandywine Creek State Park, start from the junction of U.S. 1 South (City Line Avenue) and U.S. 3 (West Chester Pike). Continue on U.S. 1 South for 17.6 miles to the town of Chadds Ford. Make a left onto Route 100 South. Watch carefully for this hard-to-see turnoff opposite the Chadds Ford Barn Shop and Inn. Drive 5.3 miles along Route 100 South until the stop sign at a four-way intersection. Hard left is Route 92 East; hard right is a continuation of Route 100 South. Straight ahead is the road for the State Park (Road 232–Adams Dam Road). Drive 0.3 miles straight ahead to the entrance for the state park on your left. Turn left and continue to bear left along the entrance road for 0.4 miles to the nature center. A one-way trip takes approximately fifty minutes.

The best time to visit Brandywine Creek State Park is during the spring landbird migration (first three weeks in May). Stop off at the nature center (closed Mondays and Tuesdays) for a map of the nature trails and a description of the park's birdlife. Tuliptree Trail, behind the nature center, is a network of foot trails through a large stand of deciduous hardwoods. Migrating and resident woodpeckers, flycatchers, thrushes, vireos, warblers, orioles, tanagers, and sparrows abound—similar to the birds seen at Ridley Creek. Below and to the right of these woods is a vast expanse of overgrown meadows and scrubby thickets. Eastern Bluebirds use the nesting boxes along the borders, while Blue-winged and Prairie Warblers, Common Yellowthroat, and Yellow-breasted Chat nest in the thickets. Indigo Bunting, American Goldfinch, and Field and Song Sparrows also favor this habitat.

During the winter months, Dark-eyed (Slate-colored) Junco and American Tree, Field, White-crowned, White-throated, Fox, and Song Sparrows can be found along the protective hedgerows.

The Brandywine Creek floodplain is crossed several times by Route 100 South between U.S. 1 South and the state park. You can also drive one-half mile past the park entrance on Road 232 to the Brandywine. Red-winged Blackbird, Yellow Warbler, Common Yellowthroat, Swamp Sparrow, and possibly Willow ("Fitz-Bew") Flycatcher nest in the vegetation bordering the creek. Flooded meadows and scattered cattail marshes along the creek provide hiding spots for Great Blue and Green Herons, Great (Common) and Cattle Egrets, and occasional Least and American Bitterns. King and Virginia Rails should also be looked for, although they are uncommon. Mallard and Wood Duck are the resident breeding ducks along the Brandywine.

The Wilmington, Delaware, Christmas Count takes in Brandywine Creek State Park, plus several other hot spots in the northern Delaware area, including Churchman's Marsh, Hoopes Reservoir, and the Delaware River. This count approaches one hundred species most years. Waterfowl (Redhead and Canvasback), raptors (Rough-legged Hawk and Northern Harrier [Marsh Hawk]), gulls, owls (Common Screech, Great Horned, Barn, and Barred), woodpeckers (Pileated and Red-headed), finches, and sparrows are tallied.

For more information, write:

Brandywine Creek State Park
P. O. Box 3782
Greenville, Del. 19807
Phone: (302) 571-3534

Map 31
Brandywine Creek State Park

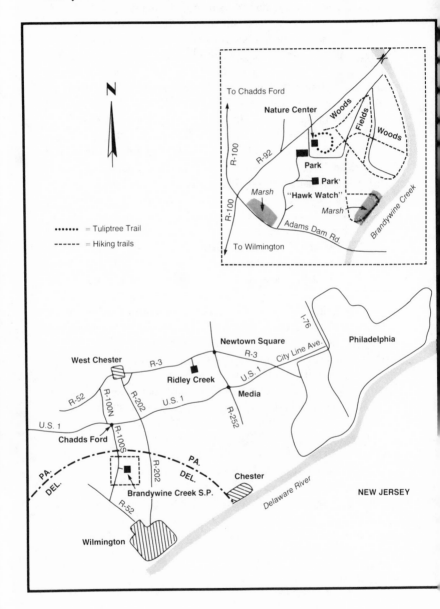

•••••• = Tuliptree Trail

- - - - - = Hiking trails

Ocean City, Maryland, Pelagic Trips

Pelagic trips to the deep waters off the Atlantic Coast allow the birdwatcher to observe highly specialized species not likely to be encountered elsewhere. Although just outside the range of this guide's coverage, the Ocean City, Maryland, Pelagic Trip is the yardstick to measure others by. Local birding clubs have sponsored other trips from the Jersey coast (i.e., Barnegat Lighthouse), but Ocean City, Maryland, has been doing it longer and more regularly. Richard A. Rowlett, who leads the Ocean City trips, is considered the dean of pelagic birding in the east. As he says in his brochure, "These trips provide the rare opportunity for those of us, who have idolized the exploits of early explorers in American Ornithology and Cetology, to be a part of our own modern day pioneering efforts to explore one of the last and long neglected frontiers of North America field biology, that of observing and establishing spatial and temporal distribution and habits of the pelagic birds and cetaceans living in the ocean waters off the middle-Atlantic States."

Ocean City, Maryland, is approximately a four-hour trip from Philadelphia. Take Route 13 South from Philadelphia (past Bombay Hook N.W.R.) to Salisbury, Maryland. Then take Route 50 East to Ocean City. You can plan a great birding weekend around the pelagic trip. Blackwater N.W.R. in Maryland, Pocomoke Swamp near Selbyville, Delaware, and Assateague Island off the Maryland-Virginia border are within easy reach.

Mr. Rowlett has consented to have portions of his 1979 brochure reprinted in this guide. The following schedule highlights the birds likely to be observed during each season.

Spring: April through June   Seven species of cetaceans were seen during this period in 1978, including Fin, Sperm, and Pilot Whales, and Risso's (Grampus), Saddle-backed, Bottle-nosed, and White-sided Dolphins. Previous years, Right, Hump-backed, and Minke Whales and Harbor Porpoises have been reported. The Baltimore Canyon area is proving to be the best and most consistent area in the northwestern Atlantic to see the odd but beautiful Risso's Dolphin!

Among seabirds, migrating tubenoses may likely include Sooty,

Greater, Cory's, and Manx Shearwaters, Northern Fulmar, Wilson's and Leach's Storm Petrels, and Northern Gannets. Carpets of Red and Northern Phalaropes often blanket the surface in late April and early May. Additional possible species include Pomarine, Parasitic, and Long-tailed Jaegers, South Polar Skua, Arctic Tern, and Sabine's Gull. In 1978, thousands of shearwaters (four species) and South Polar Skuas were seen in mid-June, and hundreds of Wilson's Storm Petrels gathered so close to our boat that we could capture them with a dip net for extra close examination of those "elusive" yellow feet!

Summer Blue Water Goodies: August and September   Late summer offers hopeful chances for tropical and sub-tropical wanderers. In the past six years, Audubon's Shearwater, Black-capped Petrel, White-faced and Band-rumped (Harcourt's) Storm Petrel, White-tailed Tropicbird, Brown Booby, Magnificent Frigatebird, and Bridled and Sooty Terns have been seen. Mind you, these are all rarities—just one or two of these would be nice. This is the best time for migrating Long-tailed Jaeger and Sabine's Gull. You can expect to see Cory's and Greater Shearwaters, phalaropes, jaegers, and perhaps a rare South Polar Skua.

Warm-water cetaceans seen in recent summers have included Spotted and Striped Dolphins, and Short-finned Pilot Whales. Also, Fin, Sei, and Minke Whales, and Bottle-nosed and Risso's Dolphins are possible. Even sea turtles, sharks, and maybe flying fish and Portuguese Man-o-war among other interesting sea life.

Baltimore Canyon Christmas Count: December   Lots and lots of birds and a real good time. Weather and water are still relatively mild if you fear a cold winter trip in February. Expected species are the same as in February, but with better chances for lingering fall migrants like Pomarine Jaeger, Greater and Manx Shearwaters, Leach's Storm Petrel, and Red Phalarope.

Albatross Weekend: February   The only mid-winter trip in 1979. It's anniversary weekend of the birth of East Coast pelagic trip mania (1973), and North America's most celebrated Yellow-nosed Albatross (1975), in addition to several other species of pelagic birds first recorded for Maryland (1973, 1974, 1975).

There will be hundreds (thousands) of birds all day. Expect hundreds of Northern Gannets and Black-legged Kittiwakes. Best chances for Northern Fulmar, Skua (Great?), Dovekie, Razorbill,

Atlantic (Common) Puffin, both Murres, and Iceland, Glaucous, and Lesser Black-backed Gulls. Additional possibilities include Manx and Greater Shearwaters, Pomarine Jaeger, Red Phalarope, Thayer's Gull, and Surprises!

Cetaceans seen in past winters have included Fin and Humpbacked Whales, Saddle-backed (Common), Bottle-nosed, and Risso's (Grampus) Dolphins. Anything is possible!

These pelagic trips sail to the Baltimore Canyon and the Outer Continental Shelf. The cost per person is $40.00 ($41.50 for the Christmas Count) for the 1979 season. The hours are from 6:00 A.M. to 6:00 P.M. (February and December) and from 6:00 A.M. to 7:00–9:00 P.M. (April through September).

For additional information and reservations write:

Richard A. Rowlett
P.O. Box 579
Ocean City, Md. 21842

Additional Delaware Hot Spots

Alapocas Woods   Near Wilmington, Delaware. Woodland birding similar to Ridley Creek State Park, Pa. Best during spring (May) migration.

Cape Henlopen State Park   Near Lewes, Del. Similar to Long Beach Island, N.J. (Barnegat Lighthouse State Park and the Holgate Unit) in both habitat and birdlife. Wintering ocean birds, gulls, and sparrows. Nesting Piping Plover, terns, and Black Skimmer. Phone: (302) 645-8983.

Churchman's Marsh   Near Newport, Delaware. Fresh-water marsh birding, including herons, egrets, bitterns, and rails.

Delaware City   Near the eastern end of the Chesapeake-Delaware Canal. Nearby Dragon Run Marsh is good for fresh-water marsh species including herons, egrets, bitterns, rails, and ducks. In past years (although not recently) a pair of Purple Gallinules had nested in the marsh. Nearby Thousand Acre Marsh is excellent for migrating shorebirds. Travel Route 9 South between Delaware City and Dover for breeding Blue Grosbeak.

Hoopes Reservoir   Northwest of Wilmington, Del. Excellent for wintering waterfowl. Much of the surrounding area is privately owned, so bird from the causeway over the reservoir.

Pea Patch Island   Fort Delaware State Park, Del. This island in the Delaware River (boat transportation is available from Delaware City, Del.) is the site of a Civil War prison and one of the largest heronries in the region. Good location for the Yellow-crowned Night Heron.

Pocomoke Swamp   Near Selbyville, Del. On the Delaware-Maryland border, Pocomoke is a three and one-half hour drive from Philadelphia. Fantastic spring landbird migration, especially warblers. Good numbers of Prothonotary, Worm-eating, Northern Parula, Yellow-throated, and Hooded Warblers. Swainson's Warbler may still nest here, although repeated use of taped calls has driven past breeders away.

Prime Hook National Wildlife Refuge   Southeast of Milford, Del., off Route 14 South. Similar to Bombay Hook. Check the swampy meadows and brackish marshes along the roads to Fowler Beach and Broadkill Beach for Black Rail, Sedge (Short-billed Marsh) Wren, and Henslow's Sparrow. American Woodcock, Chuck-will's-widow, and Whip-poor-will are present in the upland areas of the refuge. Phone: (302) 684-8419.

Redden State Forest   South of Milford, Del., off Route 113 South. Woodland birding. Good for breeding Summer Tanager. Blue Grosbeak in more open areas.

White Clay Creek Valley   North of Newark, Del. Woodland birding similar to Ridley Creek State Park, Pa. Yellow-throated and Warbling Vireos, Northern Parula, Cerulean, and Yellow-throated Warblers.

Woodland Beach Wildlife Area   East of Smyrna, Del., along Route 6 East. Similar to Bombay Hook.

Annotated Bird List
for the
Delaware Valley Region

This annotated list provides a thumbnail sketch of when and where the Delaware Valley's representative species are most likely to be seen. The main text, via the index, can be consulted for more specifics. Three hundred thirty-five species expected to occur during an average five-year period are included. Many other species, including accidentals, strays, and rarities, have also been recorded in the area. A simple listing of these birds follows the Annotated List for the sake of completeness.

Although many of the tri-state region's birds can be observed throughout the area, this list mostly limits their preferred habitats to the six major refuges and the assorted hot spots. This is in keeping with this guide's theme, "know a few good spots well." Many areas provide checklists covering the seasonal frequency of each bird recorded, thus allowing direct comparisons between refuges. Although these lists have been extensively surveyed, the probability of seeing each species is more pertinent to the birdwatcher than comparative abundance. For example, Seaside Sparrows far outnumber Purple Martins at Brigantine, but the small Martin colony is the more visible, while it's much tougher to flush the sparrows. Thus "birdability" at these various locations, not actual numbers, is reflected in the following scale:

****   Likely to be seen on at least three out of four trips during the proper season and in suitable habitat. These birds can be counted on at that location.

***   Likely to be seen on at least one out of four trips during the proper season and in suitable habitat. This is a conservative estimate, and many species are recorded more frequently. For example, when large numbers of spring warblers pour through the area on peak days in May, even uncommon species may appear more regularly than indicated.

**   Frequently present during the proper season and in suitable habitat, but requires extensive searching. If enough visits are made under favorable circumstances, the bird should be seen every year. This includes such locally common but difficult to glimpse birds as rails. Other common species may visit that location only in small numbers because of limited preferred habitat. This category also includes uncommon birds present in very small numbers at that locality.

*   Has been seen, but without the reliability of the above. This may refer to uncommon and rare species present only in very small numbers at that location, or to certain birds of irregular or cyclic occurrence, e.g., winter finches.

These ratings assume field trips of several hours. If you spend the entire day and cover most of the suitable habitat, the chances of seeing each bird are increased. Locations are listed in order of birdability, and we have attempted to include as many of the six major refuges as possible for the sake of comparison.

Also included after each bird is the relative abundance of that species, i.e., the number of birds actually present. This is designated by a five-point scale: common, moderate numbers, small numbers, very small numbers, and rare. The difference between very small numbers and rare is perhaps arbitrary. Very small numbers indicates that a few individuals are seen every year, while rare connotes that a few birds are present only in certain years. Additionally, some species are subject to recurring cyclic fluctuations in abundance, e.g., winter finches. The number of birds present may range from small to common, depending on the year and a host of other factors. This phenomenon will be covered by the term irregular after that species.

The names used for each species in this section are consistent with those recommended by the Checklist Committee of the American Birding Association (1975). Common or former names are added in parentheses as they are used in many of the standard bird-identification guides.

Common Loon   Present in small to moderate numbers in the surf along coastal locations throughout area November through April. Barnegat,*** Ocean City, N.J.,*** Cape May,*** Brigantine Island,*** and Bombay Hook** (especially Port Mahon).

Red-throated Loon   As above; more common than Common Loon.

Red-necked Grebe   Present in very small numbers along coastal inlets throughout area November through April. Abundance varies year to year. Numbers increase slightly late February through early April, when birds can also be found inland, for example at the Delaware River* behind Tinicum, Struble Lake,* and Penn Manor.*

Horned Grebe   Common in surf, bays, and inlets along coast November through April. Brigantine**** N.W.R. and Island, Barnegat,**** Cape May,**** Ocean City, N.J.,**** and Bombay Hook*** (especially Port Mahon). Occasionally inland, for example at Tinicum.*

Eared Grebe   Rare winter visitor at widely scattered coastal locations.

Pied-billed Grebe   Present year-round in moderate to common numbers on fresh-water lakes and brackish marshes throughout area. Tinicum,*** Brigantine N.W.R.,*** Cape May,*** Bombay Hook,*** Struble Lake,*** and Trenton.**

Northern Fulmar   See Pelagic Trips.

Cory's Shearwater   See Pelagic Trips.

Greater Shearwater   See Pelagic Trips.

Sooty Shearwater   See Pelagic Trips.

Manx Shearwater   See Pelagic Trips.

Leach's Storm Petrel   See Pelagic Trips.

Wilson's Storm Petrel   See Pelagic Trips.

Northern Gannet   See Pelagic Trips. Very small numbers are seen diving into the ocean, usually at a considerable distance from shore. Look for it (with scope) off Barnegat** October through April.

Great (European) Cormorant   Present in small numbers along the Jersey coast November through March. More common northward. Look for the predominately immature birds sitting on buoys off Barnegat.***

Double-crested Cormorant   Present in moderate numbers along coastal locations throughout area September through April. More common during spring (April) and fall (September–October) migrations. Barnegat,*** Ocean City, N.J.,*** Cape May,*** Brigantine*** N.W.R. and Island, and Bombay Hook*** (especially Port Mahon). Occasionally inland at the Delaware River* behind Tinicum.

Great Blue Heron   Common year-round in fresh- and salt-water marshes throughout area. Largest numbers spring through fall, with a few still present during mid-winter. Brigantine N.W.R.,**** Bombay Hook,**** Tinicum,**** Stone Harbor,**** Little Creek,**** and Cape May.****

Green Heron   Common in fresh and brackish marshes and wooded swamps throughout area April through October. Tinicum**** (along Darby Creek), Bombay Hook**** (especially Finis Pool), Manahawkin N.W.R.,**** Stone Harbor,**** Brigantine N.W.R.*** (along Doughty Creek), and Springton Reservoir*** near Ridley Creek.

Little Blue Heron   Present in moderate to common numbers in coastal marshes throughout area April through October. Stone Harbor,**** Brigantine N.W.R.,**** Bombay Hook,**** Manahawkin N.W.R.,**** Little Creek,**** and Ocean City, N.J.***

Cattle Egret   Common in coastal marshes and especially on inland livestock pastures throughout area April through October. Numbers increasing. Brigantine N.W.R.,*** Bombay Hook*** (especially along Road 85 to the refuge), King Ranch,*** Cape May*** (in pastures along the way to Higbee Beach), and Stone Harbor.**

Great (Common) Egret   Common in fresh- and salt-water marshes, especially coastal, throughout area April through October. A few remain into winter. Stone Harbor,**** Brigantine N.W.R.,**** Bombay Hook,**** Little Creek,**** Cape May,**** and Tinicum.***

Snowy Egret   Same as Great Egret.

Louisiana Heron   Same as Little Blue Heron.

Black-crowned Night Heron   Common in fresh- and salt-water marshes throughout area April through November. A few winter over. Brigantine N.W.R.,**** Stone Harbor,**** Bombay Hook,**** Manahawkin N.W.R.,**** Cape May,*** and Tinicum.***

Yellow-crowned Night Heron   Present in very small numbers in scattered brackish and salt-water marshes throughout area April through September. Look for individuals of a small breeding colony at Stone Harbor.*** Another small colony is located on Pea Patch Island*** in the Delaware River near Delaware City, Del. Breeding pairs have also been recorded at Tinicum,* Brigantine N.W.R.,* and Manahawkin N.W.R.*

Least Bittern   Present in moderate numbers but difficult to glimpse in fresh and brackish marshes throughout area April through September. Tinicum,*** Bombay Hook,*** Cape May,*** Little Creek,*** Brigantine N.W.R.,** and Trenton Marsh.**

American Bittern   Same as Least Bittern. Lesser numbers remain during winter, when brackish marshes seem to be favored: Brigantine** and Cape May.**

Glossy Ibis   Common in coastal marshes throughout area April through mid-October. Brigantine N.W.R.,**** Stone Harbor,**** Little Creek,**** Manahawkin N.W.R.,**** Cape May,*** and Ocean City, N.J.***

White Ibis   Rare late-summer straggler August through September (usually immature birds). Look for it at Stone Harbor,* also Little Creek,* Bombay Hook,* and Brigantine.*

Mute Swan   Present year-round in small numbers on scattered fresh and brackish impoundments throughout area. Brigantine N.W.R.,**** Cape May,*** Manahawkin N.W.R.,** and Bombay Hook.*

Whistling Swan   Present in small to moderate numbers on fresh and brackish impoundments throughout area October through April. Abundance varies year to year. Brigantine N.W.R.,*** Bombay Hook,*** Delaware River** behind Tinicum, Barnegat** (including Manahawkin N.W.R.), and Cape May.*

Canada Goose Common year-round in fresh and brackish marshes throughout area. Largest numbers during spring (March–April) and especially fall (October–November) migrations. Bombay Hook,**** Brigantine N.W.R.,**** Struble Lake,**** Tinicum,**** Barnegat**** (including Manahawkin N.W.R.), and Cape May.****

Brant Common in salt-water bays and inlets along coast throughout area November through April. Brigantine N.W.R.,**** Barnegat**** (bay side of Long Beach Island), Cape May,**** Cape Henlopen,*** Ocean City, N.J.,*** and Bombay Hook** (especially Port Mahon).

Greater White-fronted Goose Very small numbers (usually single birds) occur with migrating and wintering Canada Geese. Look for it around Bombay Hook* and northern Delaware.*

Snow Goose Common in coastal marshes along Jersey coast and Delaware Bay October through April. Brigantine N.W.R.,**** Bombay Hook,**** Fortescue,**** Cape May,**** and Cape Henlopen.*** Occasionally inland; Struble Lake* and French Creek S.P.* Several individuals of the Blue race are usually found among the larger Snow flocks.

Whistling (Fulvous Tree) Duck Rare late-summer straggler (sometimes in small flocks) August through September. Look for it at Bombay Hook,* also Brigantine N.W.R.* and Cape May.*

Mallard Common year-round on fresh and brackish impoundments throughout area. Brigantine N.W.R.,**** Tinicum,**** Bombay Hook,**** Cape May,**** Struble Lake,*** and Springton Reservoir*** near Ridley Creek S.P.

American Black Duck Same as Mallard. The American Black is the most common duck in salt-water marshes and bays throughout area. Barnegat**** and Ocean City, N.J.****

Gadwall Present year-round in moderate numbers in fresh and brackish marshes throughout area. Bombay Hook,**** Brigantine N.W.R.,**** Manahawkin N.W.R.,**** Tinicum,*** Cape May,*** and Struble Lake.** Largest numbers during migration.

Common Pintail Same as Gadwall. Rare during summer months. Abundant at Tinicum.****

Green-winged Teal Common in fresh and brackish marshes and lakes throughout area September through April. Tinicum,**** Brigantine N.W.R.,**** Bombay Hook,**** Manahawkin N.W.R.,**** Cape May,*** and Struble Lake.*** Singles of the Common (European) race occur in large flocks of the Green-winged. Look for it at Tinicum,* also Bombay Hook* and Brigantine N.W.R.* during the late fall.

Blue-winged Teal Present in moderate numbers in fresh and brackish marshes and lakes throughout area March through November. A few winter over. Brigantine N.W.R.,**** Bombay Hook,**** Tinicum,**** Manahawkin N.W.R.,**** Cape May,*** and Struble Lake.** Largest numbers during spring and fall migrations.

Eurasian (European) Wigeon Present in very small numbers (usually single birds) among flocks of American Wigeon October through April. Look for it during the late fall at Brigantine,* Bombay Hook,* Penn Manor,* and Tinicum.*

American Wigeon Present in moderate numbers in fresh and brackish marshes and lakes throughout area September through May. Bombay Hook,**** Brigantine N.W.R.,**** Manahawkin N.W.R.,**** Tinicum,*** Cape May,*** and Struble Lake.**

Northern Shoveler Present year-round in moderate to common numbers in fresh and brackish marshes and lakes throughout area. Peak numbers during spring and fall migrations with lesser numbers remaining to breed. Bombay Hook,**** Brigantine N.W.R.,**** Manahawkin N.W.R.,**** Tinicum,**** Cape May,*** and Struble Lake.**

Wood Duck Present in small to moderate numbers in fresh-water marshes and wooded swamps throughout area March through October. Greatest numbers at Great Swamp N.W.R.**** in northern New Jersey. A few stragglers winter over in the general area. Bombay Hook,*** Pine Barrens,*** Dragon Run Marsh*** near Delaware City, Del., Brigantine N.W.R.,** Tinicum,** Brandywine Creek S.P.,** and Ridley Creek S.P.** (nearby Springton Reservoir** should also be checked).

Redhead Present in very small numbers on fresh- and salt-water impoundments throughout area November through April. Usually seen with Canvasbacks. Look for it at Tinicum* in the late fall, also Brigantine N.W.R.,* Bombay Hook,* Penn Manor,* and Struble Lake.*

Ring-necked Duck   Present in small to moderate numbers in widely scattered localities throughout area November through April. Favors inland fresh-water lakes. Bombay Hook,*** Struble Lake,*** Tinicum,*** Penn Manor,*** Brigantine N.W.R.,** and Manahawkin N.W.R.**

Canvasback   Present in small to moderate numbers on fresh- and salt-water impoundments throughout area November through April. Greatest numbers in the Chesapeake Bay area south of the region. Tinicum** (especially on the Delaware River behind the airport), Barnegat** (including Manahawkin N.W.R.), Bombay Hook,** Penn Manor,** Brigantine N.W.R.,* and Struble Lake.*

Greater Scaup   Common in fresh, brackish, and salt water throughout area, especially coastal locations, November through April. Brigantine N.W.R.,**** Bombay Hook,**** Barnegat**** (including Manahawkin N.W.R.), Tinicum**** (including the Delaware River behind the airport), Ocean City, N.J.,**** and Cape May.****

Lesser Scaup   Present in moderate to common numbers on fresh and brackish impoundments throughout area November through April. Favors inland locales. Uncommon in areas where the Greater Scaup abounds. Look for it at Tinicum,**** Middle Creek Wildlife Management Area,**** Struble Lake,**** Penn Manor,**** on the Wilmington, Del., Christmas Count,*** Springton Reservoir*** near Ridley Creek S.P., and Churchville Reservoir.***

Common Goldeneye   Present in moderate numbers in salt-water bays and inlets throughout area November through April. Occasionally inland (Tinicum*), but favors coastal locations: Brigantine**** N.W.R. and Island, Barnegat,**** Ocean City, N.J.,*** Cape May,*** and Bombay Hook*** (especially Port Mahon).

Barrow's Goldeneye   Rare. At least one male has wintered at the Shark River Inlet,* south of Asbury Park, N.J., for the past ten years December through March.

Bufflehead   Common in fresh, brackish, and salt water throughout area, especially coastal locations, November through April.

Brigantine N.W.R.,**** Barnegat,**** Cape May,**** Bombay Hook**** (especially Port Mahon), Ocean City, N.J.,**** and Tinicum.***

Oldsquaw   Common on ocean and salt-water inlets throughout area November through early April. Barnegat,**** Ocean City, N.J.,**** Cape May,**** Brigantine Island,**** Brigantine N.W.R.,*** and Bombay Hook*** (especially Port Mahon). Occasionally inland (Delaware River* behind Tinicum).

Harlequin Duck   Present in very small numbers along coastal jetties throughout area December through March. Numbers fluctuate year to year; most likely to be seen in more northern areas. Look for it off the 8th Avenue jetty in Barnegat* and the jetties in Cape May,* Brigantine Island,* and Cape Henlopen.*

Common Eider   Same as Harlequin Duck.

King Eider   Same as Harlequin Duck.

White-winged Scoter   Common along coastal locations throughout area late September through April. Usually seen flying over the ocean in flocks or swimming off jetties. Barnegat,**** Brigantine Island,**** Cape May,**** Ocean City, N.J.,*** and Bombay Hook*** (especially Port Mahon).

Surf Scoter   Same as White-winged Scoter. Least common of the Scoter family in the general area.

Black (Common) Scoter   Same as White-winged Scoter.

Ruddy Duck   Common in fresh and brackish water throughout area October through May. A few stay the summer to breed. Tinicum**** (especially the Delaware River behind the airport), Brigantine N.W.R.,**** Bombay Hook,**** Manahawkin N.W.R.,*** Struble Lake,*** and Churchville Reservoir.***

Hooded Merganser   Present in small to moderate numbers in fresh and brackish impoundments throughout area October through April. Bombay Hook,*** Brigantine N.W.R.,*** Manahawkin N.W.R.,** Tinicum,** Middle Creek Wildlife Management Area,** and Struble Lake.*

Common Merganser   Present in moderate numbers in fresh, brackish, and (rarely) salt water throughout area November through April. Numbers increase during spring migration, especially near coast. Bombay Hook,*** Brigantine N.W.R.,*** Manahawkin N.W.R.,*** Tinicum,*** Cape May,** and Struble Lake.**

Red-breasted Merganser   Present in moderate to common numbers on ocean and salt-water inlets throughout area November through April. Barnegat,**** Cape May,**** Brigantine Island,**** Ocean City, N.J.,*** Brigantine N.W.R.,*** and Bombay Hook** (especially Port Mahon).

Turkey Vulture   Common year-round soaring above woods, meadows, and farmlands throughout area. Uncommon along the coast. Hawk Mt.,**** Bombay Hook,**** Ridley Creek,**** Brandywine Creek S.P.,**** Struble Lake,**** and Cape May.***

Black Vulture   Present year-round in small numbers in southern part of tri-state area. Look for it around Bombay Hook*** and nearby farmlands. Sightings are increasing in Lancaster, Chester, and Delaware Counties along the Pennsylvania-Delaware-Maryland borders. Recently discovered roosts are at King Ranch* and French Creek S.P.*

Northern Goshawk   Present in small numbers along mountain ridges during autumn migration (October through November). Numbers fluctuate year to year and seem to be increasing in recent years. Hawk Mt.,** Bake Oven Knob,** and Cape May.* A few birds may winter in the area, for example at Ridley Creek* and the Poconos.* Former breeder in the Poconos.

Sharp-shinned Hawk   Common along mountain ridges and along the coast during autumn migration (late September through early November). Cape May,**** Hawk Mt.,**** and Bake Oven Knob.**** Small numbers remain during the winter and can be found on most regional Christmas Counts, both inland and coastal. Poconos** breeder and rarely in southeastern Pennsylvania.*

Cooper's Hawk   Present in small numbers along coast and mountain ridges during fall migration (late September through early November). Numbers drastically reduced since late 1960s. Ratio of Cooper's to Sharpies, as well as the absolute numbers of Cooper's, are greater at Cape May*** (1:25) than at Hawk Mt.** (1:50). See *American Birds* 31 (March 1977), 157. A few Cooper's winter over and are sometimes found on regional Christmas Counts.

Red-tailed Hawk Common in woodlands and open areas throughout region October through April. Largest numbers during fall migration (October through November). Hawk Mt.,**** Bake Oven Knob,**** Bombay Hook,**** Tinicum,*** Ridley Creek,*** and Brigantine N.W.R.** A few remain to breed in the general area and the Poconos.**

Red-shouldered Hawk Present in moderate numbers along mountain ridges and coast during fall migration (October through early November). Cape May,*** Hawk Mt.,*** and Bake Oven Knob.*** A few remain to breed in the general area and the Poconos.** Small numbers winter over and can be found on many regional Christmas Counts, e.g., Bombay Hook* and Glenolden* (Tinicum).

Broad-winged Hawk Common both along mountain ridges and throughout the general area during fall migration (September through mid-October). Hawk Mt.,**** Bake Oven Knob,**** Cape May,**** and Ridley Creek.**** Present in small numbers in woodlands throughout area April through November; Bowman's Hill** and Ridley Creek.** Poconos*** breeder.

Rough-legged Hawk Present in small numbers in open, marshy areas throughout region late October through April. Bombay Hook,*** Brigantine N.W.R.,*** Manahawkin N.W.R,*** Tinicum*** (especially behind the airport), Cape May,** Hawk Mt.,* and Middle Creek Wildlife Management Area.*

Golden Eagle Small numbers (30–50) pass Hawk Mt.** and Bake Oven Knob** from late October through November. Also seen at Cape May.* A few, usually immature, individuals winter over in the general area. Brigantine N.W.R.* and the marshes near the Mullica River Estuary* are favorite locales.

Bald Eagle Small numbers (20–40) pass Hawk Mt.** and Bake Oven Knob** late August through early October. Also seen at Cape May.* A few individuals winter over—Brigantine N.W.R.* and Bombay Hook* are favorite locales. A breeding pair has been at Bombay Hook** February through April for many years.

Northern Harrier (Marsh Hawk) Present in moderate numbers in open marshy areas and farmlands throughout region late September through April. Brigantine N.W.R.,**** Bombay Hook,****

Manahawkin N.W.R.,**** Cape May,**** Tinicum**** (especially behind the airport), and Middle Creek Wildlife Management Area.*** Good concentrations pass Cape May,**** Hawk Mt.,**** and Bake Oven Knob**** September through November. May still breed in the general area, e.g., at Tinicum* and Killcohook N.W.R.*

Osprey   Moderate numbers pass Cape May,**** Hawk Mt.,*** and Bake Oven Knob*** during the fall migration (September through October). Breeds in small numbers near coastal locations late March through August—especially along the Garden State Parkway and Route 1 (Avalon Causeway) into Avalon, N.J.**** Has bred at Manahawkin N.W.R.,* Brigantine N.W.R.,* Bombay Hook,* and Prime Hook N.W.R.*

Peregrine Falcon   Present in small numbers along coastal locations and mountain ridges throughout area September through October. Best chances are at Cape May**; the Peregrine is rare at Hawk Mt.* First weekend in October is the traditional peak. Several captive-raised birds, released at Brigantine N.W.R. and Manahawkin N.W.R., are seen periodically, along with an occasional wild fall transient.

Merlin (Pigeon Hawk)   Present in small to moderate numbers along coastal locations throughout area during fall migration (September through October). Best time is first weekend in October. Cape May,*** Brigantine N.W.R.,** Manahawkin N.W.R.,** Cape Henlopen,** and Hawk Mt.*

American Kestrel (Sparrow Hawk)   Common throughout area during fall migration (September through October). Cape May, **** Hawk Mt.**** and Bake Oven Knob.**** Present in moderate numbers in open areas throughout region during colder months. Struble Lake,**** Princeton,**** Bombay Hook,*** Ridley Creek,*** Tinicum,*** and Brigantine N.W.R.** A few remain to breed during the summer.

Ruffed Grouse   Present year-round in moderate numbers in woodlands throughout northern sections of region. Most likely to be heard "drumming" during breeding season (April through June) or seen when flushed by surprise. Pine Barrens,*** Poconos,*** Hawk Mt.,** Middle Creek Wildlife Management Area,** French Creek S.P.,* and Brigantine N.W.R.*

Common Bobwhite   Present year-round in moderate numbers in open areas throughout southern sections of region. Bombay Hook*** (especially adjoining farmlands), King Ranch,*** Cape May*** (adjoining farmlands), Brigantine N.W.R.,** Brandywine Creek S.P.,** and Ridley Creek.*

Ring-necked Pheasant   Common year-round near farmlands, brushy fields, and marshes throughout area. Chester County**** (near Struble Lake), Bombay Hook**** (especially adjoining farmlands), Brandywine Creek S.P.,**** Ridley Creek,**** Tinicum,**** and Princeton.***

Wild Turkey   Present year-round in small numbers in woodlands throughout extreme northern sections of region. Poconos** and Hawk Mt.*

King Rail   Present in small to moderate numbers in fresh-water marshes throughout area April through October. Rapidly declining as a breeder and most likely seen during spring (April through mid-May) and fall (September through October) migrations. A few may winter over. Very difficult to glimpse. Bombay Hook,** Little Creek,** Trenton Marsh,** Tinicum,** and Churchman's Marsh** (near Newport, Del.).

Virginia Rail   As above. More common than King Rail, but difficult to glimpse. Also found in brackish marshes, especially during winter; Brigantine N.W.R.,* Manahawkin N.W.R.,* and Cape May.*

Clapper Rail   Common in salt and brackish marshes throughout area April through October. A few winter over. Brigantine N.W.R.,**** Manahawkin N.W.R.,**** Ocean City, N.J.,*** Nummy Island*** (near Stone Harbor Sanctuary), Tuckerton,*** and Bombay Hook*** (especially Port Mahon).

Sora   Similar to King and Virginia Rails. Small peaks during migration (April and October).

Black Rail   Present in very small numbers over widely scattered coastal locations May through October. Very difficult to glimpse. Listen for its calls between dusk and dawn. Most reliable spots in recent years have been Manahawkin N.W.R.* and Prime Hook N.W.R.* (especially along the road to Broadkill Beach). Also recorded at Brigantine N.W.R.,* Bombay Hook,* and Dividing Creek, N.J.*

Purple Gallinule   Rare. A breeding pair had been present at Dragon Run Marsh near Delaware City, Del.,** in past years (absent for the last several years). Look for this bird wandering through the Bombay Hook* and Little Creek* area during the warmer months.

Common Gallinule   Present in moderate numbers in fresh and brackish marshes throughout area April through October. Tinicum,**** Brigantine N.W.R.,*** Manahawkin N.W.R.,*** Delaware City, Del.,*** Trenton Marsh,*** and Bombay Hook.***

American Coot   Common on fresh and brackish impoundments throughout area October through May. A few remain to breed during the summer months. Brigantine N.W.R.,**** Bombay Hook, **** Manahawkin N.W.R.,*** Tinicum,*** Cape May,*** and Struble Lake.***

American Oystercatcher   Present in small to moderate numbers along coastal mudflats, protected beaches, and salt marshes throughout area March through September. Tuckerton,*** Holgate,*** Brigantine N.W.R.** and Island,** Ocean City, N.J., ** Nummy Island** near Stone Harbor Sanctuary, and Cape Henlopen.**

Semipalmated Plover   Common on tidal mudflats throughout area during spring (May) and fall (August through September) migrations. A few may linger into the colder months. Brigantine N.W.R.,**** Bombay Hook,**** Little Creek,**** Tuckerton,**** Ocean City, N.J.,**** and Tinicum*** (especially along Darby Creek).

Killdeer   Present year-round in moderate numbers on fresh and brackish mudflats and open fields throughout area. Numbers increase during spring (March through early May) and fall (August through October) migrations. Bombay Hook**** (especially adjoining farmlands), Tinicum,**** Cape May**** (especially nearby pastures), Struble Lake,*** Mercer Sod Farm,*** and Brigantine N.W.R.***

Piping Plover   Present in small numbers along coastal sandy beaches throughout area April through September. Little of the Piping Plover's breeding habitat remains undisturbed. Holgate,*** Island Beach S.P.,*** Ocean City, N.J.,*** Brigantine Island,*** Cape Henlopen,*** and Cape May.**

Lesser (American) Golden Plover   Present in small numbers in plowed fields and mudflats throughout area mid-August through early October. Rare in spring. Mercer Sod Farm,*** Bombay Hook*** (especially adjoining farmlands), Brigantine N.W.R.,** Cape May,** Tinicum,* and Princeton* (nearby sod farms).

Black-bellied Plover   Common on coastal and inland mudflats throughout area during spring (May) and fall (August through October) migrations. A few stragglers remain during winter. Brigantine N.W.R.,**** Bombay Hook,**** Tuckerton,**** Cape May,**** Tinicum,*** and Mercer Sod Farm.**

Ruddy Turnstone   Common along coastal inlets throughout area during fall (August through September) and especially spring (May through mid-June) migrations. Brigantine N.W.R.,**** Tuckerton,**** Holgate,**** Ocean City, N.J.,**** Cape May,**** and Bombay Hook*** (especially Port Mahon). A few remain during the winter.

American Woodcock   Present in moderate numbers in damp woods throughout area during spring (March through May) and fall (mid-October through November) migrations. Lesser numbers remain to breed and winter over in the region. Difficult to glimpse unless flushed by surprise or seen during the March conjugal display. Bombay Hook,*** Middle Creek Wildlife Management Area,*** Cape May*** (especially during the fall migration), Tinicum,** Ridley Creek,** and Brigantine N.W.R.*

Common Snipe   Present in moderate numbers in marshes and wet fields throughout area mid-August through May. Numbers increase during spring (March through early May) and fall (September through early November) migrations. Tinicum,*** Bombay Hook,*** Trenton Marsh,*** Middle Creek Wildlife Management Area,*** Brigantine N.W.R.,** and Cape May.**

Whimbrel   Present in moderate numbers along coastal salt marshes and mudflats throughout area during fall (August through

September) and especially spring (early April through May) migrations. Brigantine N.W.R.,*** Tuckerton,*** Manahawkin N.W.R.,*** Nummy Island*** near Stone Harbor Sanctuary, Ocean City, N.J.,** and Bombay Hook** (especially Port Mahon).

Upland Sandpiper (Plover)   Present in small numbers in open fields throughout area April through early October (becoming rare as a breeder). Most likely seen during fall (late August through mid-September) migration. Mercer Sod Farm,*** Philadelphia Airport** near Tinicum, Greater Wilmington, Del., Airport,** Bombay Hook** (especially adjoining pastures and nearby Dover Air Force Base), Cape May** (especially nearby pastures), Princeton* (nearby sod farms), and Woodstown,* N.J. (southcentral New Jersey).

Spotted Sandpiper   Present in small to moderate numbers on fresh- and salt-water ponds and streams throughout area April through early October. Most common during spring (May) and fall (mid-August through early September) migrations. Tinicum,**** Brigantine N.W.R.,*** Bombay Hook,*** Little Creek,*** Struble Lake,*** and Springton Reservoir** near Ridley Creek.

Solitary Sandpiper   Present in small numbers on fresh-water ponds and streams throughout area during spring (late April through May) and fall (mid-August through September) migrations. Tinicum,*** Poconos*** (especially Pocono Lake), Struble Lake,** Middle Creek Wildlife Management Area,** Bombay Hook,* and Brigantine N.W.R.*

Willet   Common in salt and brackish marshes throughout area April through October. Most abundant summer shorebird in the region. Brigantine N.W.R.,**** Tuckerton,**** Nummy Island**** near Stone Harbor Sanctuary, Ocean City, N.J.,**** Fortescue,**** and Bombay Hook**** (especially Port Mahon).

Greater Yellowlegs   Common along fresh-, brackish-, and salt-water edges throughout area during spring (April through May) and fall (August through October) migrations. Small numbers remain well into winter. Brigantine N.W.R.,**** Tuckerton,**** Bombay Hook,**** Nummy Island**** near Stone Harbor Sanctuary, Ocean City, N.J.,**** and Tinicum.****

Lesser Yellowlegs As Greater Yellowlegs, but somewhat less common.

Red Knot Present in small to moderate numbers along coastal inlets throughout area during spring (May) and fall (August through September) migrations. Tuckerton,*** Holgate,*** Ocean City, N.J.,*** Nummy Island,** Brigantine Island** and N.W.R.,** and Bombay Hook* (especially Port Mahon).

Purple Sandpiper Present in moderate numbers along coastal jetties throughout area November through early May. Barnegat, **** Cape May,*** Brigantine Island,*** Ocean City, N.J.,*** and Cape Henlopen.**

Pectoral Sandpiper Present in moderate numbers along coastal and inland grassy mudflats throughout area during spring (mid-April through May) and especially fall (August through early October) migrations. Bombay Hook,*** Little Creek,*** Tuckerton,*** Brigantine N.W.R.,*** Tinicum,*** and Ocean City, N.J.** Also Mercer Sod Farm.**

White-rumped Sandpiper Present in small numbers along fresh- and salt-water edges throughout area during spring (mid-May through early June) and fall (August through October) migrations. Bombay Hook,** Little Creek,** Tuckerton,** Brigantine N.W.R.,** Nummy Island,* and Tinicum.*

Baird's Sandpiper Present in very small numbers during fall (August through September) migration. Same locations as for White-rumped Sandpiper and other smaller sandpipers.

Least Sandpiper Common along coastal and inland mudflats (both fresh and salt water) throughout area during spring (May) and fall (late July through September) migrations. Brigantine N.W.R., **** Tuckerton,**** Bombay Hook,**** Little Creek,**** Nummy Island,**** and Tinicum.***

Curlew Sandpiper Rare. Search at coastal locations throughout area during spring (May) and fall (August) migrations. Tuckerton,* Brigantine N.W.R.,* Bombay Hook,* and Little Creek* are favorite stopping points, especially in late May.

Dunlin Common along coastal mudflats throughout area late September through early May. Less common inland. Brigantine

N.W.R.,**** Tuckerton,**** Bombay Hook,**** Little Creek, **** Cape May,**** and Tinicum.**

Short-billed Dowitcher   Common along coastal mudflats throughout area during spring (May) and especially fall (late July through mid-September) migrations. Less common inland. Brigantine N.W.R.,**** Tuckerton,**** Bombay Hook,**** Little Creek, **** Nummy Island,**** and Tinicum.***

Long-billed Dowitcher   Present in very small numbers in same locations as Short-billed Dowitcher. Most likely to be seen after October 1 into winter.

Stilt Sandpiper   Present in small numbers along fresh-, brackish-, and salt-water edges throughout area during fall (late July through early October) migration. More common along coast. Brigantine N.W.R.,*** Little Creek,*** Bombay Hook,** Tuckerton,** Nummy Island,** and Tinicum.**

Semipalmated Sandpiper   Similar to, but more common than, Least Sandpiper.

Western Sandpiper   Present in small to moderate numbers along coastal and inland mudflats throughout area during fall (August through October) migration. Brigantine N.W.R.,*** Tuckerton,*** Bombay Hook,*** Little Creek,*** Nummy Island,*** and Tinicum.**

Buff-breasted Sandpiper   Present in very small numbers in plowed fields, pastures, and (rarely) mudflats throughout area during fall (August through September) migration. Mercer Sod Farm,** Princeton* (nearby sod farms), Cape May* (nearby pastures), Brigantine N.W.R.,* and Philadelphia Airport* near Tinicum.

Marbled Godwit   Present in very small numbers along coastal impoundments and mudflats throughout area August through October. Numbers fluctuate year to year. Brigantine N.W.R.,** Tuckerton,* Manahawkin N.W.R.,* Nummy Island,* Cape May,* and Bombay Hook.*

Hudsonian Godwit   Present in very small numbers in fresh-, brackish-, and salt-water pools throughout area August through October. Numbers fluctuate year to year. Bombay Hook,* Little

Creek,* Brigantine N.W.R.,* Tuckerton,* Manahawkin,* and Tinicum.*

Bar-tailed Godwit   Rare visitor at coastal locations during spring (May) and fall (August through September) migrations. Has been reported at Longport, N.J.,* during mid-May for six out of the past seven years (up to 1978). Look for it working the tidal flats across from the Dunes Motel and Restaurant.

Ruff   Present in very small numbers along fresh-, brackish-, and salt-water edges throughout area May through October. Most likely seen during the spring and fall shorebird migrations. Bombay Hook,* Little Creek,* Brigantine N.W.R.,* Tuckerton,* and Tinicum* are favorite spots.

Sanderling   Common along sandy beaches and coastal mudflats throughout area late July through May. Numbers increase during spring and fall shorebird migrations, but Sanderlings are still present in good numbers during the coldest months. Barnegat,**** Brigantine Island**** and N.W.R.,**** Tuckerton,**** Cape May,**** Ocean City, N.J.,**** Bombay Hook*** (especially Port Mahon), and Tinicum.*

American Avocet   Present in small to moderate numbers along fresh and brackish ponds at a few favorite locations August through early November. Bombay Hook,*** Little Creek,*** Brigantine N.W.R.,** and Cape May.*

Black-necked Stilt   Present in small numbers at Little Creek*** late April through early September. This is the Stilt's northernmost breeding locality. Occasionally seen at Bombay Hook* and Prime Hook N.W.R.*

Red Phalarope   Present in moderate numbers offshore during spring (mid-April through May) and especially fall (September through December) migrations. Rarely found on inland ponds. See Pelagic Trips.

Wilson's Phalarope   Present in very small numbers at fresh and brackish ponds throughout area during spring (May) and fall (late July through early October) migrations. Bombay Hook,* Little Creek,* Brigantine N.W.R.,* Tuckerton,* and Tinicum* are favorite spots.

Northern Phalarope   Same as Wilson's Phalarope, but less common inland. Also seen offshore in moderate numbers. See Pelagic Trips.

Pomarine Jaeger   See Pelagic Trips.

Parasitic Jaeger   See Pelagic Trips.

Long-tailed Jaeger   See Pelagic Trips.

Skua   See Pelagic Trips. May include two separate species—the Great Skua and South Polar Skua.

Glaucous Gull   Present in very small numbers at scattered coastal locations throughout area November through early April. Look for it at Shark River Inlet,* Barnegat,* Brigantine Island,* Cape May,* and Cape Henlopen.* Occasionally inland, for example at Tinicum* and Penn Manor.* Also seen in small numbers offshore. See Pelagic Trips.

Iceland Gull   Same as Glaucous Gull.

Greater Black-backed Gull   Common at coastal locations throughout area September through May. A few summer over, with numbers increasing in recent years (has bred at Stone Harbor**). Less common inland. Barnegat,**** Brigantine N.W.R.**** and Island,**** Cape May,**** Ocean City, N.J.,**** Bombay Hook**** (especially Port Mahon), and Tinicum.***

Lesser Black-backed Gull   Rare. A few individuals are reported most years at scattered coastal locations during the colder months. Look for it at the same localities as Glaucous and Greater Black-backed Gulls. Occasionally inland (Penn Manor*).

Herring Gull   Common year-round at both coastal and inland waterways throughout area. Barnegat,**** Brigantine N.W.R.**** and Island,**** Cape May,**** Ocean City, N.J.,**** Bombay Hook,**** and Tinicum.**** Be on the lookout for the rare Thayer's Gull—now considered a separate species.

Ring-billed Gull   Same locations as, but less common than, Herring Gull. In spring flocks are frequently seen following the plow.

Black-headed Gull   Present year-round in very small numbers at widely scattered coastal locations throughout area. Most likely seen in late summer (August through October) and especially late winter–early spring (March through early May). Most productive locations seem to be northern coastal New Jersey* (north of Barnegat) and Little Creek.* A summering bird has been seen on Brigantine Island* for the past several years.

Laughing Gull Common at coastal locations throughout area April through November. Less common inland. Barnegat,**** Brigantine N.W.R.**** and Island,**** Cape May,**** Ocean City, N.J.,**** Bombay Hook**** (especially Port Mahon), and Tinicum** (especially along the Delaware River behind the airport).

Bonaparte's Gull Present in moderate numbers, often in small flocks, at coastal locations throughout area October through early May. Largest numbers during spring (April) movement. Barnegat, **** Shark River Inlet,**** Cape May,*** Bombay Hook*** (especially Port Mahon), Brigantine Island,*** and Ocean City, N.J.**

Little Gull Present year-round in very small numbers at widely scattered coastal locations throughout area. Usually seen in late winter–early spring (March through early May). Most productive spots seem to be northern coastal New Jersey* (north of Barnegat) and especially the Little Creek** area. There were flocks of up to forty birds at Little Creek in April during the mid-1970s.

Black-legged Kittiwake Rare. Occasionally seen from shore at scattered coastal locations throughout area November through March. Look for it at the same locations as for Glaucous and Greater Black-backed Gulls. Most likely seen on winter Pelagic Trips.

Gull-billed Tern Present in small numbers at coastal locations, especially in southern parts of area, May through September. Numbers are increasing, with a trend toward northern expansion. Little Creek,*** Prime Hook N.W.R.,*** Bombay Hook,** Brigantine N.W.R.,** and Nummy Island.*

Forster's Tern Present in moderate to common numbers in brackish, fresh-, and salt-water marshes throughout area late April through October. Greatest numbers along coast—occasionally inland (Tinicum*). Brigantine N.W.R.,**** Manahawkin N.W.R., **** Little Creek,**** Bombay Hook,**** Cape May,**** and Ocean City, N.J.***

Common Tern   Common along coastal beaches, inlets, and salt-water marshes throughout area April through October. Barnegat, **** Holgate,**** Brigantine Island**** and N.W.R.,*** Ocean City, N.J.,**** Cape May,**** and Bombay Hook*** (especially Port Mahon).

Roseate Tern   Rare now, but formerly nested on outer sandy beaches and islands (Holgate*). A breeding pair was present there in 1978. Last stronghold seems to be Long Island, N.Y.***

Little (Least) Tern   Common (but recently declining) along coastal inlets and brackish and salt-water marshes throughout area May through September. Brigantine N.W.R.,**** Manahawkin N.W.R.,**** Holgate,**** Ocean City, N.J.,**** Little Creek, **** Cape May,**** and Bombay Hook.***

Royal Tern   Present in small numbers along coastal beaches throughout area May through mid-October. Most likely seen during late summer (August through September), when numbers increase (and sometimes large congregations form) along coastal points. Holgate,*** Cape Henlopen,*** Cape May,*** Brigantine Island,** Ocean City, N.J.,* and Bombay Hook* (especially Port Mahon).

Caspian Tern   Present in very small numbers at scattered coastal locations throughout area, usually during late summer (August through September). Look for it at Holgate,** Brigantine N.W.R.,* Cape May,* Little Creek,* Cape Henlopen,* and Bombay Hook.* Occasionally inland (Tinicum*).

Black Tern   Present in small to moderate numbers at coastal locations throughout area during spring (April through mid-May) and especially fall (mid-July through September) migrations. Little Creek,*** Brigantine N.W.R.,** Manahawkin N.W.R.,** Holgate,** Cape Henlopen,** and Bombay Hook.** Occasionally inland (Tinicum*).

Black Skimmer   Common along coastal bays, inlets, and salt-water marshes throughout area May through early October. Holgate,**** Nummy Island,**** Ocean City, N.J.,**** Tuckerton,**** Brigantine Island*** and N.W.R.,*** Cape May,*** and Bombay Hook** (especially Port Mahon).

Razorbill   See Pelagic Trips.

Thin-billed (Common) Murre   See Pelagic Trips.

Thick-billed Murre   See Pelagic Trips.

Dovekie   See Pelagic Trips.

Black Guillemot   See Pelagic Trips.

Atlantic (Common) Puffin   See Pelagic Trips.

Rock Dove (Pigeon)   Common year-round in urban, suburban, and farming areas throughout region.

Mourning Dove   Common year-round in open fields, farmlands, and suburban areas throughout region. Ridley Creek S.P.,**** Struble Lake,**** Tinicum,**** Bombay Hook,**** Cape May,**** and Brigantine N.W.R.***

Monk Parakeet   Rare now due to extermination. Scattered nesting records throughout area during early 1970s.

Yellow-billed Cuckoo   Present in small to moderate numbers in woodlands and marshy thickets throughout area late April through September. Secretive and hard to glimpse. Numbers fluctuate from year to year depending on caterpillar infestations. Most frequently seen during spring (May) migration. Bombay Hook,** Ridley Creek** (including Tyler Arboretum), Brandywine Creek S.P.,** Tinicum,** Wissahickon,** and Brigantine N.W.R.*

Black-billed Cuckoo   Same as, but less common than, Yellow-billed Cuckoo.

Barn Owl   Present year-round in small to moderate numbers near farmlands and open woodlands throughout area. Nocturnal. Most frequently seen during Christmas Counts, when it may roost in tree groves. Bombay Hook,** Churchville Reservoir,** Upper, Middle, and Lower Bucks County, Pa., Christmas Counts** (see *American Birds*, July issues), Princeton,** Tinicum,* and Wilmington, Del., Christmas Count.*

Common Screech Owl   Common year-round in woodlands, and even suburban plots, throughout area. Nocturnal. Good numbers on most regional Christmas Counts. Wilmington, Del., Christmas Count,*** Upper, Middle, and Lower Bucks County, Pa., Christmas Counts*** (see *American Birds*, July issues), Bombay Hook, *** Ridley Creek,*** Princeton,*** and Tinicum.**

Great Horned Owl   Present year-round in moderate numbers in large woodlands throughout area. Nocturnal. Good numbers on most regional Christmas Counts, but generally less common than Screech Owl. Bombay Hook,*** Wilmington, Del., Christmas Count,*** Bucks County, Pa., Christmas Counts,*** Ridley Creek,*** Princeton,*** and Brigantine N.W.R.**

Snowy Owl   Rare. Many winters a few individuals are reported in open areas (fields, marshes, etc.) throughout region. The Snowy's numbers fluctuate year to year, but it is never common or regular. Brigantine N.W.R.* and Island,* Manahawkin N.W.R.,* Tuckerton,* Island Beach S.P.,* and Tinicum* (especially the nearby airport) are favorite haunts.

Barred Owl   Present year-round in small numbers in wet deciduous woodlands throughout area. Nocturnal. Bombay Hook** and Little Creek** are most likely spots. Also occasionally seen (heard) at Brandywine Creek S.P.,* on the Wilmington, Del., Christmas Count,* Trenton Marsh,* Poconos* (especially Pocono Lake), and White Clay Creek, Del.* (near Newark, Del.).

Long-eared Owl   Present in small to moderate numbers in woodlands, especially evergreen stands, throughout area November through March. Breeds rarely in the general region. Churchville Reservoir,** Princeton,** National Park, N.J.,** Upper, Middle, and Lower Bucks County, Pa., Christmas Counts** (see *American Birds*, July issues), Lancaster County, Pa., Christmas Count* (near Millersville, Pa.), and Tinicum.*

Short-eared Owl   Present in small to moderate numbers in open fields and marshes throughout area October through March. A few may still breed in the general region during the warmer months (Philadelphia Airport* near Tinicum). Diurnal. Manahawkin N.W.R.*** and Barnegat Marshes,*** Tuckerton,** Tinicum** (especially near the airport), Brigantine N.W.R.,** Killcohook N.W.R.,** and Bombay Hook** (especially Port Mahon).

Saw-whet Owl   Present in very small numbers in thickets and evergreen stands throughout area November through April. Small breeding populations in the Poconos* and Pine Barrens* during the warmer months. Nocturnal. Individual birds are tallied on such regional Christmas Counts as Princeton,* Tinicum,* Brigantine N.W.R.,* Bucks County, Pa.,* and Bombay Hook* (including

Little Creek). The best location to see this owl during the winter months is Thorofare, N.J.** This small town is located near Paulsboro off Route 295 on the way to the Delaware Memorial Bridge from Camden.

Chuck-will's-widow   Present in small numbers in southern New Jersey pinelands late April through September. Most frequently heard at dusk or dawn in the area around Leeds Point,*** near Brigantine N.W.R. Leeds Eco-trail and Lily Lake Road (within the N.W.R.) and Leeds Point Road (northwest of the N.W.R.) are favorite locations. Less common than Whip-poor-will in these areas. Has recently nested at Dividing Creek, N.J.*

Whip-poor-will   Present in moderate to common numbers in scrubby deciduous and pine woods throughout area late April through September. Nocturnal. Most common in Pine Barrens**** (Wharton Tract) and in pine-oak woods along Jersey coast, i.e., Leeds Point,**** Brigantine N.W.R.,**** and Manhawkin N.W.R.**** Hawk Mt.*** and Poconos*** are best inland locations.

Common Nighthawk   Moderate numbers are seen hawking insects at dusk over cities and towns throughout area May through September. Largest numbers and most frequently seen during fall (August through September) migration. Philadelphia*** (especially lighted areas like Veteran's Stadium and racetracks), Tinicum,*** Pine Barrens,*** Ridley Creek,*** Wissahickon,*** Brigantine N.W.R.,** and Bombay Hook.*

Chimney Swift   Commonly seen hawking insects at dusk over cities and towns throughout area mid-April through September. Philadelphia,**** Tinicum,**** Ridley Creek,**** Wissahickon,**** Bombay Hook,*** and Brigantine N.W.R.***

Ruby-throated Hummingbird   Present in moderate numbers in flower gardens and open woodlands throughout area during spring (May) and fall (late August through September) migrations. A few remain to breed during the summer. Hawk Mt.*** (September), Bombay Hook,*** Ridley Creek,*** Wissahickon,*** Tinicum,** and Brigantine N.W.R.*

Belted Kingfisher   Present in moderate numbers near fresh and salt water throughout area April through October. A few winter over. Brigantine N.W.R.,*** Bombay Hook,*** Tinicum,*** Brandywine Creek S.P.,*** Cape May,*** and Ridley Creek.***

Common (Yellow-shafted) Flicker   Common in open woodlands and along field borders throughout area April through October. Lesser numbers winter over. Ridley Creek**** (including Tyler Arboretum), Wissahickon,**** Cape May**** (especially during fall), Bombay Hook,**** Brigantine N.W.R.,*** and Tinicum.***

Pileated Woodpecker   Present year-round in very small numbers in large woodlands throughout area, especially in northern sections of the region. Poconos,** Hawk Mt.,** Bowman's Hill,** and French Creek S.P.* Occasionally seen farther south, especially during colder months; i.e., Ridley Creek,* Princeton,* Glenolden Christmas Count,* Wissahickon,* and Brandywine Creek S.P.*

Red-bellied Woodpecker   Present year-round in moderate numbers in woodlands throughout area. Numbers gradually increasing with range expansion northward. Brandywine Creek S.P.,**** Bombay Hook,**** Ridley Creek,*** Wissahickon,*** Princeton,*** and Brigantine N.W.R.*

Red-headed Woodpecker   Present year-round in very small numbers in a few open woodlands throughout area. A small breeding colony (two to four pairs) remains at Cape May Courthouse, N.J.*** Look for it at Hawk Mt.** during fall migration and in Lancaster County, Pa.,* in scattered tree groves during the colder months. Individual birds have been reported on several regional Christmas Counts, including Wilmington, Del., Christmas Count,* Bombay Hook,* Bucks County, Pa.,* and Cape May.*

Yellow-bellied Sapsucker   Present in small to moderate numbers in open woodlands throughout area during fall (late September through November) migration. A few winter over, and another small peak occurs in early spring (April). Wissahickon,*** Ridley Creek,*** Hawk Mt.,*** Cape May,** Poconos,** and Bombay Hook.* Individual birds are reported on several regional Christmas counts.

Hairy Woodpecker   Present year-round in moderate numbers in woodlands throughout area. Ridley Creek,*** Wissahickon,***

Bombay Hook,*** Princeton,*** Brandywine Creek S.P.,*** and Brigantine N.W.R.**

Downy Woodpecker Common year-round in woodlands throughout area. Ridley Creek,**** Wissahickon,**** Bombay Hook, **** Princeton,**** Brigantine N.W.R.,*** and Tinicum.***

Eastern Kingbird Common near farmlands, roadsides, and open woodlands throughout area May through September. Ridley Creek**** (especially Tyler Arboretum), Bombay Hook,**** Brandywine Creek S.P.,**** Cape May**** (August-September), Tinicum,*** and Brigantine N.W.R.***

Western Kingbird Very small numbers are reported annually along the Jersey coast during fall (late August through October) migration. Look for it at Cape May,** Brigantine N.W.R.,* and Long Beach Island, N.J.*

Great Crested Flycatcher Present in moderate to common numbers in deciduous woodlands throughout area May through early September. Ridley Creek**** (especially Tyler Arboretum), Bombay Hook,**** Brandywine Creek S.P.,**** Wissahickon, **** Princeton,*** Brigantine N.W.R.,** and Tinicum.**

Eastern Phoebe Present in moderate numbers in open woodlands and meadows near water throughout area April through September. Favors bridges and abandoned buildings. Ridley Creek,**** Wissahickon,*** Bowman's Hill,*** Bombay Hook,*** Brandywine Creek S.P.,*** Princeton,*** and Tinicum.**

Yellow-bellied Flycatcher Present in very small numbers throughout area during spring (late May) and especially fall (September) migrations. Prefers quiet woodlands, but can be seen along marshy borders at coastal locations during fall movement. Look for it at Tinicum,* Ridley Creek,* Brigantine N.W.R.,* and Cape May.*

Acadian Flycatcher Present in moderate numbers in deciduous woodlands, often near water, throughout area May through early September. Largest numbers during spring (May) migration. Prefers inland locations; rare in New Jersey. Ridley Creek,**** Brandywine Creek S.P.,*** Wissahickon,*** Bombay Hook,*** Hay Creek,*** and Bull's Island, N.J.,** near Bowman's Hill.

Traill's Flycatcher   Present in moderate numbers near streams and marshes throughout area mid-May through early September. Prefers willow and alder thickets. Now considered two separate species: Willow Flycatcher ("Fitz-Bew") and Alder Flycatcher ("Fee-Bee'-o"). The relative status of the two new species is still unclear. Willow seems the far more common breeding bird in the area. Tinicum**** (despite the Tinicum checklist noting the Alder as most common), Trenton Marsh,**** Bombay Hook,** Ridley Creek S.P.,** Brandywine Creek S.P.,** Middle Creek Wildlife Management Area,** and Brigantine N.W.R.* (bred recently). The Poconos*** (Long Pond) seem to be ideal habitat for the Alder species.

Least Flycatcher   Present in small to moderate numbers in open woodlands and orchards throughout northern sections of the region May through early September. Poconos,*** Hawk Mt.,*** Hay Creek** near Reading, Pa., and Ridley Creek.* Present in small to moderate numbers throughout region during spring (May) and fall (late August through mid-September) migrations. Wissahickon,*** Ridley Creek,** Princeton,** Bowman's Hill,** Bombay Hook,* and Tinicum.*

Eastern Pewee (Eastern Wood Pewee)   Present in moderate numbers in woodlands throughout area mid-May through September. Ridley Creek,**** Wissahickon,**** Bombay Hook,*** Brandywine Creek S.P.,*** Princeton,*** Bowman's Hill,*** and Brigantine N.W.R.**

Olive-sided Flycatcher   Present in very small numbers throughout area during spring (May) and especially fall (late August through September) migrations. Favors dead treetops near water. Look for it at Poconos,* Hawk Mt.,* Ridley Creek,* Bombay Hook,* Wissahickon,* and Bowman's Hill.* Probably a rare Poconos breeder.

Horned Lark   Present in moderate numbers in open fields, plowed farmlands, and ocean dunes throughout area October through May. A few remain to breed in the region (mid-March through June). Bombay Hook*** (especially adjoining farmlands), King Ranch*** (and surrounding Chester County, Pa., farmlands), Long Beach Island*** (Holgate and Barnegat), Brigantine Island,*** Mercer Sod Farm,*** Cape May,*** and Tinicum** (especially near the airport).

Tree Swallow   Common in open areas near water throughout region April through October. Numbers greatly increase during fall (late August through September) migration, especially along the coast. Bombay Hook,**** Brigantine N.W.R.,**** Cape May**** (especially in fall), Tinicum,**** Struble Lake,**** and Ridley Creek*** (especially Tyler Arboretum). A few remain into the colder months, especially during milder winters.

Bank Swallow   Present in moderate numbers in open areas near gravel banks throughout region mid-April through mid-September. Largest numbers during spring (May) and fall (August) migrations. Bombay Hook,**** Tinicum,*** Cape May*** (especially in fall), Brigantine N.W.R.,** and Struble Lake.**

Rough-winged Swallow   Present in small to moderate numbers near water (usually fresh water) throughout area during spring (mid-April through May) and fall (August) migrations. Largest numbers during spring migration; a few remain to breed. Tinicum,*** Ridley Creek,*** Cape May,*** Struble Lake,** Bombay Hook,** and Brigantine N.W.R.*

Barn Swallow   Common in open areas throughout region mid-April through September. Bombay Hook,**** Brandywine Creek S.P.,**** Struble Lake,**** Ridley Creek,**** Brigantine N.W.R.,**** and Tinicum.****

Cliff Swallow   Present in small numbers in open areas, especially near buildings, throughout region during spring (May) and fall (August through early September) migrations. Look for it with other swallows during migration at Struble Lake,** Cape May,* Tinicum,* Princeton* (especially near Wargo Road Watershed), and Bombay Hook.* A few scattered breeding colonies remain in the area (West Chester, Pa.,** and Lake Ontelaunee** near Reading, Pa.). Poconos** are still most reliable breeding location.

Purple Martin   Present in moderate numbers, especially at "martin apartment houses," throughout area mid-April through mid-September. Seen with the other swallows hawking insects over bodies of water during migration. Brigantine N.W.R.,**** Bombay Hook,**** Aston Mills, Delaware County, Pa.,**** Cape May,*** Struble Lake,** and Tinicum.**

Blue Jay   Common year-round in woodlands, brushy borders, and suburbs throughout area. Ridley Creek,**** Brigantine

N.W.R.,**** Bombay Hook,**** Wissahickon,**** Princeton, **** Cape May,**** and Tinicum.***

Northern (Common) Raven   Rare. In recent years increasingly seen in Poconos* area and Hawk Mt.* late fall through early spring.

American (Common) Crow   Common year-round in open woodlands, farmlands, and suburbs throughout area. Ridley Creek,**** Bombay Hook,**** Princeton,**** Hawk Mt.,**** Tinicum,**** Cape May,**** and Brigantine N.W.R.***

Fish Crow   Present year-round in moderate to common numbers near large bodies of water (both salt and fresh) throughout area. Lesser numbers during winter, when Fish Crows may be greatly outnumbered by the American Crow—even along the coast. Brigantine N.W.R.,**** Manahawkin N.W.R.,**** Tinicum**** (including the Delaware River behind the airport), on the Wilmington, Del., Christmas Count,**** Bombay Hook**** (especially the Port Mahon–Little Creek area), and Cape May.***

Black-capped Chickadee   Common in open woodlands, along brushy borders, and at feeders north of the Philadelphia-Trenton axis October through mid-April. Princeton,**** Bucks County, Pa.**** (Upper, Middle, and Lower Christmas Counts), Ridley Creek,**** Tinicum,*** and Brandywine Creek S.P.** Breeding occurs in northern sections of the region, e.g., Poconos,**** Hawk Mt.,**** and Bowman's Hill.***

Carolina Chickadee   Common year-round in open woodlands, along brushy borders, and at feeders south of the Philadelphia-Trenton axis. The breeding chickadee of the Philadelphia area and southwards. Some overlap with the Black-capped during winter in the Philadelphia area. Brigantine N.W.R.,**** Ridley Creek,**** Bombay Hook,**** Princeton,**** Brandywine Creek S.P.,**** and Tinicum.***

Boreal Chickadee   Rare winter visitor to feeders in northern sections of the region.

Tufted Titmouse   Common year-round in open woodlands, along brushy borders, and at feeders throughout area. Ridley Creek,**** Hawk Mt.,**** Princeton,**** Wissahickon,**** Bombay Hook,**** Brigantine N.W.R.,*** and Tinicum.***

White-breasted Nuthatch Present year-round in moderate to common numbers in woodlands and near suet feeders throughout area. Greatest numbers during colder months, with a few breeders remaining during the summer. Ridley Creek,**** Hawk Mt.,**** Princeton,**** Wissahickon,**** Brigantine N.W.R.,*** Bombay Hook,*** and Tinicum.**

Red-breasted Nuthatch Present in small numbers in coniferous woods and near suet feeders throughout area October through April. Abundance varies year to year; may be almost common during invasion years. Poconos** breeder. Pine Barrens,** Ridley Creek,** Princeton,** Hawk Mt.,** on the Wilmington, Del., Christmas Count,* Brigantine N.W.R.,* and Bombay Hook.*

Brown-headed Nuthatch Very small numbers are recorded in the extreme southern part of the region. Reported yearly by the Rehoboth, Del., Christmas Count** (where it occurs year-round) and occasionally from the Cape Henlopen–Prime Hook, Del., Count.*

Brown Creeper Present in small to moderate numbers in woodlands throughout area October through April. Poconos breeder.** Pine Barrens,*** Ridley Creek,*** Princeton,*** on the Wilmington, Del., Christmas Count,*** Hawk Mt.,*** Bombay Hook,** and Brigantine N.W.R.**

House Wren Present in moderate to common numbers along woodland edges, brushy borders, and gardens throughout area mid-April through early October. Bombay Hook,*** Ridley Creek*** (especially Tyler Arboretum), Brandywine Creek S.P.,*** Wissahickon,*** Princeton,*** Tinicum,*** and Brigantine N.W.R.**

Winter Wren Present in small numbers in wet, brushy woodlands throughout area October through late April. Secretive. Largest numbers during spring (early April) and fall (late October through mid-November) migrations. Poconos* breeder. Ridley Creek,*** Tinicum,** Princeton,** Wissahickon,** Trenton Marsh,** Bombay Hook,** and on the Wilmington, Del., Christmas Count.**

Carolina Wren Present year-round in moderate to common numbers in brushy woodlands throughout area. Lesser numbers remain during colder months, with many being killed by severe winters. Bombay Hook,*** Brandywine Creek S.P.,*** Ridley Creek,*** Wissahickon,*** Princeton,*** Tinicum,*** and Brigantine N.W.R.**

Marsh (Long-billed Marsh) Wren   Present in moderate numbers in cattail marshes throughout area late April through early October. Tinicum,*** Brigantine N.W.R.,*** Bombay Hook,*** Trenton Marsh,*** Dragon Run Marsh** near Delaware City, Del., and Churchman's Marsh** near Newport, Del.

Sedge (Short-billed Marsh) Wren   Present in very small numbers in sedge marshes and wet meadows in widely scattered localities throughout region late April through early October. Gone from most former haunts; the marshes adjoining the Delaware Bay are the only remaining spots where breeding probably still occurs. Individual wintering birds are occasionally reported on several Christmas Counts in southern parts of the region (e.g., Bombay Hook* and Cape Henlopen–Prime Hook, Del.*). Look for it in Maryland** (Elliot, Assateague, and Kent Islands), Prime Hook N.W.R.** (along Fowler Beach and Broadkill Beach Roads), Little Creek,* Bombay Hook* (Bear Swamp Pool), and Dividing Creek, N.J.*

Northern Mockingbird   Common year-round in thickets, brushy woodland borders, and suburbs throughout area. Ridley Creek, **** Bombay Hook,**** Brandywine Creek S.P.,**** Tinicum,**** Brigantine N.W.R.,**** and Cape May.****

Gray Catbird   Common in thickets, brushy woodland borders, and suburbs throughout area mid-April through October. A few stragglers remain during the winter. Ridley Creek,**** Bombay Hook,**** Brandywine Creek S.P.,**** Wissahickon,**** Brigantine N.W.R.,**** and Tinicum.****

Brown Thrasher   Similar to, but less common than, Gray Catbird. Quieter than previous two species and more likely to be overlooked. Three asterisks instead of four for Brown Thrasher at Gray Catbird locations.

American Robin   Common on suburban lawns, fields, and wooded edges throughout area mid-March through October. Many individuals from farther north winter over in moist woods—often in large flocks. Ridley Creek**** (especially Tyler Arboretum),

Bombay Hook,**** Brandywine Creek S.P.,**** Wissahickon, **** Brigantine N.W.R.,**** and Tinicum.****

Wood Thrush   Common in deciduous woodlands throughout area late April through mid-October. Ridley Creek,**** Bombay Hook,**** Wissahickon,**** Princeton,**** Brandywine Creek S.P.,**** Brigantine N.W.R.,** and Tinicum.**

Hermit Thrush   Present in moderate to common numbers in deciduous woodlands and thickets throughout area during spring (April through early May) and fall (October through early November) migrations. A few individuals winter over in the region. Poconos*** breeder. Bombay Hook,**** Ridley Creek,**** Wissahickon,**** Princeton,**** Brandywine Creek S.P.,**** Brigantine N.W.R.,** and Tinicum.***

Swainson's (Olive-backed) Thrush   Common in deciduous woodlands throughout area during spring (May) and fall (September through October) migrations. Bombay Hook,**** Ridley Creek,**** Wissahickon,**** Princeton,**** Brandywine Creek S.P.,**** Brigantine N.W.R.,** and Tinicum.**

Gray-cheeked Thrush   Like Swainson's, but present only in small to moderate numbers. One less asterisk for the Gray-cheeked at each of the Swainson's localities.

Veery   Common in moist, deciduous woodlands throughout area during spring (May) and fall (September through mid-October) migrations. Moderate numbers remain to breed at inland localities. Ridley Creek,**** Brandywine Creek S.P.,**** Wissahickon,**** Princeton,**** Bombay Hook,**** Brigantine N.W.R.,** and Tinicum.**

Eastern Bluebird   Present year-round in small numbers in open woodlands, farms, and orchards throughout area. Numbers seem to have increased over the past five years due to erection of nesting boxes. Most frequently seen in countryside west of Philadelphia. Small peaks during spring (mid-March through April) and fall (October) migrations. Tyler Arboretum*** (near Ridley Creek), Longwood Gardens*** (near Kennett Square, Pa.), Princeton,** Audubon Wildlife Sanctuary** (near Valley Forge S.P.), Poconos,** Pine Barrens,** and Hawk Mt.**

Blue-gray Gnatcatcher   Present in moderate numbers in wet, deciduous woodlands throughout area mid-April through September. Ridley Creek,**** Wissahickon,*** Bowman's Hill,*** Princeton,*** Brandywine Creek S.P.,*** Bombay Hook,** and Brigantine N.W.R.*

Golden-crowned Kinglet   Present in moderate numbers in woodlands, especially those with conifers, throughout area October through April. Peak numbers during spring (March through April) and fall (October through November) migrations. Poconos** breeder. Brigantine N.W.R.,*** Hawk Mt.,*** Ridley Creek,*** Wissahickon,*** Princeton,*** Brandywine Creek S.P.,*** Bombay Hook,** and Tinicum.**

Ruby-crowned Kinglet   Similar to Golden-crowned.

Water Pipit   Present in small to moderate numbers in plowed fields and grassy meadows throughout area late September through April. Peak numbers during October-November fall migration. Bombay Hook*** (especially adjoining farmlands), Struble Lake*** (especially adjoining farmlands), King Ranch,*** Mercer Sod Farm,*** Cape May*** (especially adjoining pastures and farmlands), and Tinicum** (especially near the airport).

Cedar Waxwing   Present in moderate numbers along wooded edges and orchards throughout area during spring (May) and especially fall (September through October) migrations. Ridley Creek, *** Hawk Mt.*** (especially in fall), Brandywine Creek S.P.,*** Wissahickon,*** Princeton,** Tinicum,** and Bombay Hook.** Poconos breeder.*** Erratic but good numbers usually remain during the winter months and appear on regional Christmas Counts.

Northern Shrike   A rare winter visitor to northern sections of the region. Prefers open countryside, occasionally coastal marshes. Individual birds are occasionally seen on several regional Christmas Counts, e.g., Princeton.*

Loggerhead Shrike   Present in very small numbers in open, partially wooded areas throughout region late August through mid-April. Small peaks during spring (March) and especially fall (September through October) migrations. Abundance has sharply declined in the past decade. Look for it at Bombay Hook** (reported annually on Christmas Count), Cape May,* Tinicum,*

Princeton,* and Struble Lake* (especially surrounding country-side).

European Starling Common year-round in urban, suburban, farming, and wooded areas throughout region.

White-eyed Vireo Present in moderate to common numbers in dense, wet thickets throughout area mid-April through October. Brigantine N.W.R.,**** Brandywine Creek S.P.,**** Ridley Creek**** (including Tyler Arboretum), Bombay Hook,*** Tinicum,*** and Princeton.***

Yellow-throated Vireo Present in small numbers in deciduous woodlands near water throughout area May through September. Most likely seen during spring (May) migration. Ridley Creek,*** Princeton,*** Bombay Hook,** Brandywine Creek S.P.,** Hay Creek** (near Reading, Pa.), Bowman's Hill,** and Wissahickon.*

Solitary Vireo Present in small to moderate numbers in deciduous woodlands throughout area during spring (mid-April through early May) and fall (September through October) migrations. Most frequently seen during spring migration. Poconos breeder.*** Wissahickon,*** Princeton,*** Bombay Hook,** Ridley Creek,** Bowman's Hill,** Brandywine Creek S.P.,** and Brigantine N.W.R.*

Red-eyed Vireo Common in deciduous woodlands throughout area May through mid-October. Ridley Creek,**** Wissahickon, **** Princeton,**** Bombay Hook,**** Bowman's Hill,**** Brigantine N.W.R.,*** and Tinicum.**

Philadelphia Vireo Present in very small numbers in woodlands (prefers lower-middle stories) throughout area during spring (May) and especially fall (September through early October) migrations. Same locations as other vireos.

Warbling Vireo Present in small numbers in mature shade trees near water throughout area May through mid-September. Ridley Creek,*** Brandywine Creek S.P.,** Princeton,** Bowman's Hill,** Tinicum,* and Wissahickon.*

Black-and-white Warbler Common in deciduous woodlands throughout area during spring (late April through May) and fall

(late August through September) migrations. Ridley Creek,****
Wissahickon,**** Princeton,**** Bowman's Hill,**** Hawk
Mt.,**** Brigantine N.W.R.,**** Bombay Hook,**** and Tini-
cum.*** Poconos*** breeder. Local breeding sites in the general
area include Pine Barrens,* Brigantine N.W.R.,* and Ridley
Creek.*

Prothonotary Warbler   Present in small numbers in swampy
woodlands in southern parts of the region May through August.
Look for it in Great Cedar Swamp, Cape May County, N.J.,***
Pine Barrens,** Bombay Hook** (especially Finis Pool), Dividing
Creek, Cumberland County, N.J.,** Princeton,* and Bull's Is-
land* (near Bowman's Hill).

Worm-eating Warbler   Present in small numbers in dry, thick
woodlands throughout area May through mid-September. Most
likely seen during spring (May) migration. Look for it during migration at Hawk Mt.,*** Bowman's Hill,** Wissahickon,** Ridley Creek** (especially Tyler Arboretum), Princeton,** Brandywine Creek S.P.,* and Bombay Hook.* A few local breeders may
remain in suitable habitat, e.g., Hawk Mt.,** Bowman's Hill,*
Hay Creek,* and Ridley Creek.* Poconos** breeder.

Golden-winged Warbler   Present in very small numbers in
open, scrubby woodlands throughout area during spring (May) and
fall (mid-August through September) migrations. Look for it in
same localities as Blue-winged during migration. Wissahickon**
is an especially good spot. Poconos** breeder (especially the
P.E.E.C.). Local breeding may occur in northern sections of the
region; Hawk Mt.* and Reading, Pa.*

Blue-winged Warbler   Present in moderate to common numbers
in open, scrubby woodlands and brushy fields throughout area May
through early September. Ridley Creek,**** Brandywine Creek
S.P.,**** Princeton**** (especially Wargo Road area), Wissahickon,*** Brigantine N.W.R.,*** Bombay Hook,** and Tinicum.** Hybrids between Golden-winged and Blue-winged Warblers (Brewster's and the rare Lawrence's) are occasionally seen in
the area, usually at the above locations.

Tennessee Warbler   Present in small to moderate numbers in
deciduous woodlands (upper story) throughout area during spring
(May) and fall (late August through September) migrations. Cape

May,*** Wissahickon,*** Bowman's Hill,*** Ridley Creek,** Brandywine Creek S.P.,** Princeton,** Bombay Hook,** and Brigantine N.W.R.*

Orange-crowned Warbler   Present in very small numbers in brushy tangles throughout area during spring (May) and especially fall (mid-September through early November) migrations. Most likely seen after October 1, and easily confused with several other species. Look for it at Tinicum,* Princeton,* and Cape May.*

Nashville Warbler   Present in small to moderate numbers along scrubby woodland edges throughout area during spring (May) and fall (September through mid-October) migrations. Cape May, *** Brigantine N.W.R.,*** Princeton,*** Ridley Creek,** Brandywine Creek S.P.,** Bombay Hook,* and Tinicum.* Erratic breeder in suitable habitat in northern sections of the region (Hawk Mt.* and Poconos*).

Northern Parula Warbler   Present in moderate to common numbers in moist, deciduous woodlands throughout area during spring (May) and fall (September through early October) migrations. Erratic breeder in suitable habitat. Ridley Creek,**** Wissahickon,**** Princeton,**** Bowman's Hill,**** Brigantine N.W.R.,*** Bombay Hook,*** and Tinicum.**

Yellow Warbler   Common in wet, brushy areas (both fresh and salt water) throughout region May through September. Brigantine N.W.R.,**** Tinicum,**** Bombay Hook,**** Trenton Marsh, **** Cape May,**** Ridley Creek,**** and Brandywine Creek S.P.***

Magnolia Warbler   Present in moderate numbers in deciduous woodlands throughout area during spring (May) and fall (late August through September) migrations. Poconos*** breeder. Wissahickon,**** Ridley Creek,*** Princeton,*** Bowman's Hill,*** Bombay Hook,*** Brigantine N.W.R.,*** and Tinicum.**

Cape May Warbler   Present in small numbers in woodlands (especially those with evergreens) and brushy tangles throughout area during spring (May) and especially fall (September through mid-October) migrations. Tinicum** (especially fall), Wissahickon,** Princeton,** Ridley Creek,* Bombay Hook,* Cape May,* Bowman's Hill,* and Brigantine N.W.R.*

Black-throated Blue Warbler   Present in moderate numbers in deciduous woodlands (prefers lower story) throughout area during spring (May) and fall (September through mid-October) migrations. Poconos** breeder. Wissahickon,**** Ridley Creek,*** Princeton,*** Bowman's Hill,*** Bombay Hook,*** Brigantine N.W.R.,** and Tinicum.**

Yellow-rumped (Myrtle) Warbler   Common in woodlands and brushy edges throughout area during spring (mid-April through May) and fall (mid-September through October) migrations. One of the earliest spring migrants; a few individuals winter over, especially near the coast where they may be common during mild winters. Poconos** breeder. Ridley Creek,**** Wissahickon,**** Princeton,**** Bowman's Hill,**** Brigantine N.W.R.,**** Bombay Hook,**** Tinicum,**** and Cape May.****

Black-throated Green Warbler   Similar to, but more common than, Black-throated Blue, both during migration and on Poconos*** breeding grounds. Prefers middle and upper woodland stories. Local breeding population in the Pine Barrens.*

Cerulean Warbler   Present in small numbers in deciduous woodlands (prefers upper story) throughout area May through mid-September. Ridley Creek,*** Brandywine Creek S.P.,** Hay Creek,** Wissahickon,** Bowman's Hill,* and Princeton.*

Blackburnian Warbler   Present in moderate numbers in deciduous woodlands throughout area during spring (May) and fall (late August through early October) migrations. Poconos*** breeder. Ridley Creek,*** Wissahickon,*** Princeton,*** Bowman's Hill,*** Bombay Hook,** Brigantine N.W.R.,** and Tinicum.*

Yellow-throated Warbler   Present in very small numbers in deciduous woodlands near water (prefers sycamores) in scattered localities throughout area May through August. Commoner southward, e.g., Pocomoke Swamp, Del.*** Look for it on Bull's Island, N.J.,** Dividing Creek, Cumberland County, N.J.,* Hay Creek* near Reading, Pa., and Ridley Creek.*

Chestnut-sided Warbler   Present in moderate numbers in open woodlands in brushy edges throughout area May through September. Most frequently seen during spring (May) and fall (late August through September) migrations. Ridley Creek,**** Brandywine Creek S.P.,**** Princeton,*** Wissahickon,*** Bombay Hook,*** Tinicum,** and Brigantine N.W.R.*

Bay-breasted Warbler   Present in small to moderate numbers in woodlands throughout area during spring (May) and fall (September through early October) migrations. Wissahickon,**** Princeton,*** Ridley Creek,*** Bowman's Hill,*** Bombay Hook,** Tinicum,* and Brigantine N.W.R.*

Blackpoll Warbler   Present in moderate to common numbers in woodlands throughout area during spring (mid-May through early June) and fall (September through mid-October) migrations. Wissahickon,**** Ridley Creek,*** Princeton,*** Bowman's Hill,*** Bombay Hook,*** Brigantine N.W.R.,*** and Tinicum.**

Pine Warbler   Present in moderate numbers in woodlands mixed with pines throughout area during spring (April through early May) and fall (late August through mid-October) migrations. One of the earliest spring migrants. Pine Barrens,**** Brigantine N.W.R.,*** Ridley Creek** (especially Tyler Arboretum's Pinetum), Bowman's Hill,** Brandywine Creek S.P.,** Bombay Hook,* and Wissahickon.* Common breeder in large evergreen tracts, e.g., Pine Barrens.****

Prairie Warbler   Present in moderate to common numbers in scrubby meadows throughout area late April through September. Ridley Creek,**** Pine Barrens,**** Brandywine Creek S.P.,**** Brigantine N.W.R.,*** Cape May,*** Princeton*** (especially Wargo Road Watershed area), Bombay Hook,** and Tinicum.**

Palm Warbler   Present in moderate to common numbers in open woodlands (prefers lower story) and brushy edges throughout area during spring (April through early May) and fall (mid-September through October) migrations. One of the earliest spring migrants. A few winter over. Cape May**** (especially near dunes during fall), Ridley Creek,*** Tinicum,*** Princeton,*** Bombay Hook,*** Wissahickon,*** and Brigantine N.W.R.**

Ovenbird   Common in deciduous woodlands (prefers ground and lower story) throughout area late April through October. Peak numbers during spring (May) and fall (September through mid-Octo-

ber) migrations. Ridley Creek,**** Wissahickon,**** Princeton,**** Bowman's Hill,**** Brigantine N.W.R.,*** Bombay
Hook,*** and Tinicum** (during migration).

Northern Waterthrush   Present in moderate numbers in swampy
woodlands and along streams throughout area during spring (mid-
April through May) and fall (late August through early October)
migrations. Poconos* breeder. Brigantine N.W.R.,*** Tinicum,*** Bombay Hook,*** Wissahickon,*** Ridley Creek,***
Princeton,*** and Bowman's Hill.***

Louisiana Waterthrush   Present in moderate numbers in
swampy woodlands and especially along streams throughout area
mid-April through early September. Most likely seen during spring
(mid-April through May) and fall (August through early September) migrations. One of the earliest spring migrants. Ridley
Creek,*** Wissahickon*** (especially along the creek), Bowman's Hill,*** Hawk Mt.,*** Princeton,*** Bombay Hook,**
and Tinicum.*

Kentucky Warbler   Present in moderate numbers in thick under-
growth of moist, deciduous woodlands throughout area May
through early September. Ridley Creek*** (especially Tyler
Arboretum), Princeton,*** Bombay Hook,*** Brandywine Creek
S.P.,*** Bowman's Hill,*** and Wissahickon.***

Connecticut Warbler   Present in very small numbers during fall
(September through October) migration. Rarely observed during
spring (May) migration. Favors brushy tangles. Look for it at
Princeton,** Cape May,** Tinicum,* Brigantine N.W.R.,* and
Ridley Creek.*

Mourning Warbler   Present in very small numbers during late
spring (late May through mid-June) and fall (late August through
mid-October) migrations. Latest and rarest of the spring migrants.
Same habitat and locations as Connecticut Warbler. Former Poconos breeder.

Common Yellowthroat   Common in brushy tangles and open,
moist woodlands throughout area mid-April through early October.
A few individuals may remain during milder winters. Ridley
Creek,**** Brigantine N.W.R.,**** Tinicum,**** Bombay
Hook,**** Wissahickon,**** Cape May,**** and Princeton****
(especially Wargo Road area).

Yellow-breasted Chat   Present in small to moderate numbers in dense thickets (often with scattered saplings) throughout area May through September. Most frequently seen during spring (May) migration; a few individuals may remain during milder winters. This species is probably on the decline, but local populations vary widely in numbers. Ridley Creek,*** Brandywine Creek S.P.,*** Cape May,*** Bombay Hook,** Princeton** (especially Wargo Road area), Tinicum,** and Brigantine N.W.R.**

Hooded Warbler   Present in small numbers in understory of moist, deciduous woodlands throughout area May through mid-September. More likely heard than seen. Hawk Mt.,*** Pine Barrens** (especially in woodlands south and east of the Barrens proper), Ridley Creek,** Brigantine N.W.R.,** Princeton,** Hay Creek,* Bombay Hook,* and Wissahickon.*

Wilson's Warbler   Present in small numbers in brushy tangles near water throughout area during spring (mid-May through mid-June) and fall (late August through September) migrations. One of the latest spring migrants. Look for it at Tinicum,** Cape May,** Brigantine N.W.R.,** Ridley Creek,** Princeton,** Bombay Hook,* and Wissahickon.*

Canada Warbler   Present in moderate to common numbers in lower story of deciduous woodlands throughout area during spring (May) and fall (mid-August through late September) migrations. Poconos** breeder. Wissahickon,**** Ridley Creek,**** Princeton,**** Bowman's Hill,**** Bombay Hook,*** Brigantine N.W.R.,*** and Tinicum.**

American Redstart   Common in deciduous woodlands throughout area during spring (late April through May) and fall (late August through early October) migrations. Moderate numbers remain to breed in the region. Ridley Creek,**** Wissahickon,**** Princeton,**** Bowman's Hill,**** Bombay Hook,**** Brigantine N.W.R.,*** and Tinicum.***

House Sparrow   Common year-round in cities, suburbs, farmlands, and open woodlands throughout area.

Bobolink   Present in moderate numbers in grassy fields and marshes (both salt and fresh) throughout area during spring (May) and especially fall (mid-August through early October) migrations. Most likely seen during fall movement when in their drab, brown-

yellow "reedbird" plumage. Tinicum,*** Brigantine N.W.R.,***
Cape May,*** Bombay Hook,*** Chester County, Pa., farmlands*** (e.g., Doe Run), Manahawkin N.W.R.,*** and Princeton.** There are a few small breeding colonies widely scattered
throughout the region, e.g., King Ranch*** near Unionville, Pa.,
and Princeton.**

Eastern Meadowlark   Common in grassy fields, pastures, and
marshy borders throughout area mid-March through October.
Moderate numbers remain during colder months (November
through March). Bombay Hook,**** Struble Lake**** (especially adjoining farmlands), Cape May,**** Brigantine N.W.R.,
*** Ridley Creek*** (especially Tyler Arboretum), and Tinicum*** (especially near the airport).

Yellow-headed Blackbird   Rare. A few stragglers (usually immatures and females) show up most years at regional marshes from
late summer (August) into the colder months. Look for it at Brigantine N.W.R.,* Bombay Hook,* Little Creek,* Cape May,* and
the Odessa to Wilmington, Del., area.*

Red-winged Blackbird   Common year-round in meadows,
swamps, and farmlands throughout area. Greatest numbers during
spring (March) and fall (September through mid-November) migrations. Brigantine N.W.R.,**** Bombay Hook,**** Tinicum,**** Cape May,**** Struble Lake**** (especially adjoining
farmlands), Princeton*** (especially Wargo Road area), and
Ridley Creek.***

Orchard Oriole   Present in small numbers along wooded edges in
rural and farming areas throughout region May through August.
Prefers large shade trees. Ridley Creek,*** Princeton** (especially Wargo Road area), Cape May,** Brandywine Creek S.P.,**
Bombay Hook,** Chester County, Pa.** (especially near Struble
Lake and Unionville), Tinicum,* and Wissahickon* (especially
near Bells Mill Road).

Northern (Baltimore) Oriole   Present in moderate to common
numbers in open woodlands and along wooded edges in rural and
farming areas throughout region May through September. Most
likely seen during spring (May) and fall (late August through September) migrations. Ridley Creek,**** Wissahickon,**** Prince-

ton,**** Bowman's Hill,**** Tinicum,*** Bombay Hook,**
and Brigantine N.W.R.*

Rusty Blackbird Present in small to moderate numbers in
swampy woodlands and brushy fields near water throughout area
mid-October through early May. Tinicum,**** Trenton Marsh,
*** Bombay Hook,*** Cape May,*** on the Wilmington, Del.,
Christmas Count,*** Chester County, Pa.** (near Struble Lake
and Unionville), and Brigantine N.W.R.*

Brewer's Blackbird Rare. Individual birds are sometimes reported in widely scattered localities throughout the region during
the winter months, usually in mixed flocks of blackbirds. For the
past twenty-five years, a small flock of up to two dozen birds has
visited the farms near Bombay Hook**—Burrough's pig farm being a favorite. The birds arrive in early November and remain
through March.

Boat-tailed Grackle Present year-round in small to moderate
numbers in tidal salt-water marshes in southern parts of the region.
Little Creek,*** Bombay Hook,*** Cape May,*** Fortescue,***
Ocean City, N.J.,** and Brigantine N.W.R.** Good Christmas
Counts of this species for the past several years in the above locales.

Common Grackle Common year-round in suburbs, farmlands,
open woodlands, and marshy areas throughout region. Largest
numbers appear during spring (March through April) and fall (September through November) migrations; numbers decrease during
the coldest months. Bombay Hook,**** Brigantine N.W.R.,****
Cape May,**** Tinicum,**** Brandywine Creek S.P.,**** and
Ridley Creek.****

Brown-headed Cowbird Present year-round in moderate numbers in suburbs, farmlands, open woodlands, and marshy areas
throughout region. Largest numbers appear during spring (March
through April) and fall (September through mid-November) migrations. The reduced winter population frequently visits feeders.
Bombay Hook,**** Chester County, Pa., farmlands,**** Cape
May**** (especially adjoining pastures), Brandywine Creek
S.P.,**** Tinicum,*** Ridley Creek,*** and Brigantine
N.W.R.**

Scarlet Tanager   Present in moderate to common numbers in deciduous woodlands throughout area during spring (May) and fall (September through early October) migrations. Lesser numbers remain to breed in suitable habitat. Wissahickon,**** Ridley Creek,**** Princeton,**** Bowman's Hill,**** Bombay Hook, *** Brigantine N.W.R.,** and Tinicum.**

Summer Tanager   Present in very small numbers in mixed pine-hardwood forests in southern parts of the region May through early October. Numbers seem to be gradually increasing. Look for it at Redden State Forest, Del.,*** Dividing Creek, Cumberland County, N.J.,* and Parvin S.P., Salem County, N.J.*

Northern Cardinal   Common year-round in suburbs, brushy tangles, and open woodlands throughout area. Ridley Creek,**** Wissahickon,**** Princeton,**** Bombay Hook,**** Brigantine N.W.R.,**** Tinicum,**** and Bowman's Hill.****

Rose-breasted Grosbeak   Present in moderate numbers in deciduous woodlands throughout area during spring (May) and fall (late August through early October) migrations. Wissahickon,**** Ridley Creek,*** Princeton,*** Bowman's Hill,*** Tinicum,*** Bombay Hook,** and Brigantine N.W.R.** Lesser numbers remain to breed in northern sections (Bowman's Hill** and Hay Creek**).

Blue Grosbeak   Present in small numbers in hedgerows adjacent to weedy fields in widely scattered localities throughout area May through September. Very local, more common southwards. Redden State Forest,*** Assunpink Game Management Area** near Trenton, N.J., Bombay Hook,** and Tinicum* (especially behind Philadelphia Airport). The rural and farming areas along Route 9 South*** between Delaware City, Del., and Little Creek, Del., are the most promising locations.

Indigo Bunting   Present in moderate to common numbers in hedgerows adjacent to brushy fields and wooded edges throughout area mid-May through September. Tinicum*** (especially behind Philadelphia Airport), Bombay Hook,*** Brandywine Creek S.P.,*** Princeton*** (especially Wargo Road area), Chester County, Pa.*** (near Struble Lake), Ridley Creek*** (especially Tyler Arboretum), and Brigantine N.W.R.**

Dickcissel Rare. Favors grassy fields, coastal locations, and feeders. Look for it at Island Beach S.P.,* Long Beach Island,* Brigantine N.W.R.,* and Cape May,* during the fall and early winter.

Evening Grosbeak An irregular winter visitor (October through April) to feeders and wooded edges (especially with evergreens) throughout area. Numbers fluctuate widely year to year, with greatest numbers occurring in northern sections of the region—Poconos,** Hawk Mt.,** and Pine Barrens.** During invasion years, this bird is seen at many refuges and birding hot spots throughout the region.

Purple Finch Present in small to moderate numbers at feeders and along wooded edges throughout area mid-October through April. Poconos*** breeder. Area feeders,*** Hawk Mt.,*** Ridley Creek*** (especially Tyler Arboretum), Brandywine Creek S.P.,*** Princeton,*** Tinicum,** Bombay Hook,** and Brigantine N.W.R.**

House Finch Common at feeders and along brushy wooded edges throughout area mid-October through April. Numbers and range are rapidly increasing, as is summer nesting. Same locations as Purple Finch, with the House Finch the much commoner species (add one asterisk per locale).

Pine Grosbeak Rare winter visitor (November through March) to area feeders and evergreen stands. Occurrence is unpredictable year to year, with most sightings in northern sections of the region. Look for it in the Poconos* and at Hawk Mt.* during the winter months.

Common Redpoll Irregular winter visitor (November through March) to feeders, hedgerows, and weedy fields throughout area. Numbers fluctuate widely year to year; the Redpoll may be common during invasion years. Look for it in northern sections of the region (Hawk Mt.* and Poconos*). During invasion years it may be present at feeders and various birding hot spots throughout the region. Search each flock for the very rarely seen Hoary Redpoll.

Pine Siskin Irregular winter visitor (October through April) to feeders, wooded edges, and evergreen stands throughout area. Numbers fluctuate widely year to year; some individuals are present most years. May be common during invasion years. Occasional Poconos* breeder. Look for it in northern sections of the region (Hawk Mt.,** Poconos,** and Pine Barrens**). During invasion years is found at feeders and such birding hot spots as Princeton,* Brandywine Creek S.P.,* Bombay Hook,* Brigantine N.W.R.,* and Ridley Creek.*

American Goldfinch   Common year-round in weedy fields, hedgerows, and wooded edges throughout area. Visits feeders during winter. Ridley Creek,**** Bombay Hook,**** Brandy-wine Creek S.P.,**** Tinicum**** (especially behind the air-port), Princeton**** (especially Wargo Road area), Chester County, Pa.**** (near Struble Lake), and Brigantine N.W.R.***

Red Crossbill   Irregular winter visitor (November through April) to evergreen stands throughout area. Numbers fluctuate widely year to year and seems more common in northern sections of the region (Hawk Mt.* and Poconos*). Look for it during invasion years in Pine Barrens,* Ridley Creek* (especially Tyler Arboretum Pinetum), and Brigantine N.W.R.*

White-winged Crossbill   Same locations as Red Crossbill, but more scarce.

Rufous-sided Towhee   Present in moderate to common numbers in brushy thickets throughout area mid-April through October. Small numbers remain during winter. Ridley Creek,**** Brandy-wine Creek S.P.,**** Pine Barrens,**** Princeton,**** Bombay Hook,**** Wissahickon,*** Brigantine N.W.R.,*** and Tini-cum.***

Ipswich Sparrow   Present in small numbers in coastal dunes throughout area mid-November through March. Now considered a subspecies of the Savannah. Look for it while walking through the dunes on Long Beach Island*** (Barnegat Lighthouse S.P. and Holgate Unit), Brigantine Island,** Ocean City, N.J.,** Cape May,** and Cape Henlopen.**

Savannah Sparrow   Present in moderate to common numbers in grassy fields and marshes (both salt and fresh water) throughout area during spring (mid-March through May) and fall (September through November) migrations. Fair numbers remain during win-ter, and a few individuals stay on to breed during the summer months in suitable habitat (e.g., Unionville, Pa.**). Bombay

Hook,**** Brigantine N.W.R.,**** Tuckerton,**** Holgate,**** Cape May,**** Chester County, Pa.**** (near Unionville), and Tinicum.***

Grasshopper Sparrow   Present in small numbers in dry grassy fields throughout area mid-April through early October. May be locally common, but is more often heard than seen. Numbers increase during spring (mid-April through mid-May) and fall (late August through early October) migrations. NAFEC*** (Air Force Base at Pomona, N.J., near Brigantine N.W.R.), Chester County, Pa.*** (between Doe Run and Unionville), Bombay Hook,** Route 9 South** between Delaware City, Del., and Little Creek, Del., Princeton** (especially Wargo Road area), and Pennypack Park.*

Henslow's Sparrow   Rare in old weedy fields in widely scattered locales throughout region mid-April through early October. Gone from past breeding spots in the area. Most likely seen in Maryland** (Elliot, Assateague, and Kent Islands). Locally, look for it at Prime Hook N.W.R.* (along Fowler Beach and Broadkill Beach Roads), Little Creek* (along Road 349), and Bombay Hook.* Has also been recorded (although rarely) at Princeton* (Wargo Road area) and near Unionville, Pa.*

Sharp-tailed Sparrow   Common in salt and brackish marshes throughout area mid-April through early October. A few individuals winter over. Most reliably seen when flushed while combing cordgrass salt meadows. Brigantine N.W.R.,*** Manahawkin N.W.R.,*** Tuckerton,*** Bombay Hook,*** Holgate,*** Ocean City, N.J.,*** and Nummy Island*** (near Stone Harbor Sanctuary).

Seaside Sparrow   Same as Sharp-tailed Sparrow. Slightly less common, and prefers cordgrass salt meadows with scattered bushes and reeds.

Vesper Sparrow   Present in very small numbers in meadows, open roadsides, and along field borders in scattered localities throughout area April through early November. Most frequently seen during spring (April through early May) and fall (September through early November) migrations. A few birds remain during the winter months. Look for it in the foothills and pastures below Hawk Mt.,** Poconos,** Chester County, Pa.* (near Unionville),

Princeton* (especially Wargo Road area), Tinicum,* NAFEC* near Pomona, N.J., and various regional Christmas Counts.

Lark and Clay-colored Sparrows   Very small numbers are recorded annually during fall migration along coastal locations, especially at Cape May.*

Dark-eyed (Slate-colored) Junco   Common in suburbs, brushy fields, and wooded margins throughout area mid-October through April. Poconos*** breeder. Ridley Creek**** (especially Tyler Arboretum), Brandywine Creek S.P.,**** Bombay Hook,**** Tinicum,**** Princeton**** (especially Wargo Road area), and Brigantine N.W.R.**** Search each group of birds for the rarely seen Oregon Junco, which is now considered a subspecies.

American Tree Sparrow   Present in moderate numbers to common in brushy fields, hedgerows, and wooded edges throughout area mid-October through mid-April. Tinicum,**** Brandywine Creek S.P.,**** Bombay Hook,**** Chester County, Pa.**** (near Struble Lake), Princeton**** (especially Wargo Road area), Ridley Creek,**** and Brigantine N.W.R.***

Chipping Sparrow   Present in moderate numbers along wooded edges and open meadows (or lawns) with scattered trees throughout area April through mid-October. Ridley Creek*** (especially Tyler Arboretum), Brandywine Creek S.P.,*** Bombay Hook,*** Princeton*** (especially Wargo Road area), Chester County, Pa.*** (near Unionville), Bowman's Hill*** (especially nearby open areas of Washington Crossing S.P.), and Brigantine N.W.R.**

Field Sparrow   Present in moderate numbers in weedy fields and along hedgerows throughout area April through October. Largest numbers during spring (April through early May) and fall (September through October) migrations. A few remain during winter months. Bombay Hook,*** Brandywine Creek S.P.,*** Ridley Creek*** (including Tyler Arboretum), Princeton*** (especially Wargo Road area), Chester County, Pa.*** (near Struble Lake), Tinicum,*** and Brigantine N.W.R.**

White-crowned Sparrow   Present in small numbers in hedgerows and brushy thickets throughout area October through early May. Abundance fluctuates year to year. Tinicum,** Brandywine Creek S.P.,** Bombay Hook,** Princeton** (especially Wargo Road area), Chester County, Pa.** (near Struble Lake), Cape May,** and Ridley Creek.*

White-throated Sparrow   Common in brushy thickets, woodland floors, and near feeders throughout area mid-September through early May. Poconos*** breeder. Ridley Creek,**** Brandywine Creek S.P.,**** Tinicum,**** Princeton,**** Bombay Hook, **** Wissahickon,**** and Brigantine N.W.R.****

Fox Sparrow   Present in small to moderate numbers in wet, brushy thickets throughout area mid-October through mid-April. Most commonly seen during spring (March through mid-April) and fall (mid-October through November) migrations. Tinicum,*** Cape May,*** Princeton,*** Bombay Hook,*** Brandywine Creek S.P.,** Ridley Creek,** Wissahickon,** and Brigantine N.W.R.**

Lincoln's Sparrow   Present in very small numbers in brushy thickets and moist woodlands throughout area during spring (late March through early May) and especially fall (September through October) migrations. Look for it in same locales as the White-crowned, White-throated, and Fox Sparrows.

Swamp Sparrow   Present in moderate numbers in fresh-water marshes and along creeks throughout area early April through October. Largest numbers during spring (mid-April through mid-May) and fall (mid-September through October) migrations. Fair numbers remain locally during winter months. Tinicum,*** Bombay Hook,*** Brandywine Creek S.P.,*** Cape May,*** Princeton,*** Ridley Creek,** and Brigantine N.W.R.**

Song Sparrow   Common year-round in brushy thickets, swampy borders, and wooded edges throughout area. Peak numbers during spring (late March through April) migration. Tinicum,**** Bombay Hook,**** Brandywine Creek S.P.,**** Ridley Creek,**** Princeton**** (especially Wargo Road area), Cape May,**** Brigantine N.W.R.,**** and Wissahickon.***

Lapland Longspur   Present in very small numbers in open fields, plowed farmlands, and beach edges throughout area November through April. Usually seen with Horned Larks and Snow Buntings at the same localities listed for those species.

Snow Bunting   Present in small numbers in open fields, plowed farmlands, and beach edges at widely scattered locales throughout area mid-October through March. Abundance and location vary from year to year, with some flocks of up to several hundred birds. Look for it at Tinicum* (especially behind the airport), Long Beach Island* (Barnegat Lighthouse S.P. and Holgate), Chester County, Pa.* (near Struble Lake and Unionville), Cape May,* Brigantine N.W.R.* and Island,* Cape Henlopen,* Bombay Hook,* and Princeton* (especially Wargo Road area).

Accidental Species

This section includes vagrant species that have occurred in the Delaware Valley region at least once over the past two decades. Although not exhaustive, this list should alert the birder to the wealth of possibilities in the area.

Arctic Loon

Western Grebe

Black-browed Albatross

Yellow-nosed Albatross
  (Ocean City, Md., Pelagic
  Trip)

Audubon's Shearwater

White-faced Storm Petrel
  (Ocean City, Md., Pelagic
  Trip)

Black-capped Petrel (Ocean
  City, Md., Pelagic Trip)

Band-rumped (Harcourt's)
  Storm Petrel (Ocean City,
  Md., Pelagic Trip)

White-tailed Tropicbird (Ocean
  City, Md., Pelagic Trip)

American White Pelican

Brown Pelican

Brown Booby (Ocean City,
  Md., Pelagic Trip)

Anhinga

Magnificent Frigatebird

Wood Stork (Ibis)

White-faced Ibis

American Flamingo (escapee?)

Black Brant

Barnacle Goose

Lesser White-fronted Goose

Ross' Goose

Cinnamon Teal

Tufted Duck

Common Shelduck (escapee?)

Ruddy Shelduck (escapee?)

Swallow-tailed Kite

Mississippi Kite

Swainson's Hawk

Ferruginous Hawk

Gyrfalcon

Eurasian (European) Kestrel

Chukar (introduced)

Sandhill Crane

Yellow Rail

Wilson's Plover

Black-tailed Godwit

Spotted Redshank

European Jacksnipe (Great
  Snipe)

Thayer's Gull

Franklin's Gull

Sabine's Gull (Ocean City,
   Md., Pelagic Trip)
Arctic Tern
Sooty Tern
Bridled Tern
Sandwich Tern
White-winged Black Tern
Noddy Tern
Common Ground Dove
Rufous Hummingbird
Red-shafted Flicker (now sub-
   species of Common Flicker)
Black-backed Three-toed
   Woodpecker
Fork-tailed Flycatcher
Scissor-tailed Flycatcher
Greater Kiskadee (Flycatcher)
Weid's Crested Flycatcher
Say's Phoebe
Black-billed Magpie
Bewick's Wren
Varied Thrush
Northern Wheatear

Sprague's Pipit
Bohemian Waxwing
Swainson's Warbler
Virginia's Warbler
Audubon's Warbler (now sub-
   species of Yellow-rumped
   Warbler)
Black-throated Gray Warbler
Townsend's Warbler
Western Meadowlark
Bullock's Oriole (now sub-
   species of Northern Oriole)
Western Tanager
Black-headed Grosbeak
Painted Bunting
Hoary Redpoll
Green-tailed Towhee
Lark Bunting
Oregon Junco (now subspecies
   of Dark-eyed Junco)
Harris' Sparrow
Golden-crowned Sparrow

Bibliography and References

This short bibliography includes texts, guides, and journals covering the haunts and characteristics of birds known to the Delaware Valley region. Some will help familiarize the reader with local birding clubs and fellow birders.

American Birds. Published bimonthly by the National Audubon Society, 950 Third Avenue, New York, N.Y., 10022.

Birding. Published bimonthly by the American Birding Association, Box 4335, Austin, Tex., 78765.

Brady, Alan, et al. *A Field List of Birds of the Delaware Valley Region*. Philadelphia, Pa.: Delaware Valley Ornithological Club, 1972. Available from the Academy of Natural Sciences of Philadelphia, 19th and the Parkway, Philadelphia, Pa., 19103.

Brett, James J., and Alexander C. Nagy. *Feathers in the Wind*. Kempton, Pa.: Hawk Mountain Sanctuary Association, 1973.

Cassinia. Published annually by the Delaware Valley Ornithological Club, Academy of Natural Sciences of Philadelphia, 19th and the Parkway, Philadelphia, Pa., 19103.

Delmarva Ornithological Society. *Where to Look for Birds on the Delmarva Peninsula*. (D.O.S. monograph No. 2). Greenville, Del.: Delmarva Ornithological Society, 1978.

The Delmarva Ornithologist. Published biannually by the Delmarva Ornithological Society, Box 4247, Greenville, Del., 19807.

Fables, David. *Annotated List of New Jersey Birds*. Newark, N.J.: Urner Ornithological Club, 1955.

Fleming, Lorraine M. *Delaware's Outstanding Natural Areas and Their Preservation*. Hockessin, Del.: Delaware Nature Education Society, 1978.

Geffen, Alice. *A Birdwatcher's Guide to the Eastern United States*. Woodbury, N.J.: Barron's Educational Series, 1978.

Harrison, George H. *Roger Tory Peterson's Dozen Birding Hot Spots*. New York, N.Y.: Simon and Schuster, 1976.

Heintzelman, Donald S. *A Guide to Eastern Hawk Watching*. University Park, Pa.: Pennsylvania State University Press, 1976.

———. *Autumn Hawk Flights: The Migrations in Eastern North America*. New Brunswick, N.J.: Rutgers University Press, 1975.

Leck, Charles. *Birds of New Jersey: Their Habits and Habitats*. New Brunswick, N.J.: Rutgers University Press, 1975.

New Jersey Audubon. Published monthly by the New Jersey Audubon Society, 790 Ewing Avenue, Franklin Lakes, N.J., 07417.

Pettingill, Olin S., ed. *The Bird Watcher's America*. New York, N.Y.: Thomas Y. Crowell, 1965.

———. *A Guide to Bird Finding: East of the Mississippi*. 2nd ed. New York, N.Y.: Oxford University Press, 1977.

Piatt, Jean. *Adventures in Birding: Confessions of a Lister*. New York, N.Y.: Alfred A. Knopf, 1973.

Poole, Earl L. *Pennsylvania Birds: An Annotated List*. Philadelphia, Pa.: Delaware Valley Ornithological Club, 1964. Available from the Academy of Natural Sciences of Philadelphia, 19th and the Parkway, Philadelphia, Pa., 19103.

Rickert, Jon E. *A Guide to North American Bird Clubs*. Elizabethtown, Ky.: Avian Publications, 1978.

Stone, Witmer. *Bird Studies at Old Cape May*. 2 vols. Philadelphia, Pa.: Delaware Valley Ornithological Club, 1937 (out of print). Reprint, New York, N.Y.: Dover Publications, 1965.

Street, Phillips B. "Birds of the Pocono Mountains, 1890–1954." *Cassinia* 41 (1954): 3–76.

———. "Birds of the Pocono Mountains, 1955–1975." *Cassinia* 55 (1974–1975): 3–16.

Summit Nature Club. *Field Trip Guide*. Summit, N.J.: Summit Nature Club, 1979.

Tahoma Audubon Society. *Nature Guide (1978–1979)*. Available from Nature Guide, 34915 4th Avenue South, Federal Way, Wash., 98003.

West Chester Bird Club. *Annotated List of Chester County Birds* (1979). Available from the West Chester Bird Club, Box 62, Westtown, Pa., 19395.

Wood, Merrill. *Birds of Pennsylvania: When and Where to Find Them*. Rev. ed. University Park, Pa.: Pennsylvania State University, Agricultural Experiment Station, 1973.

Index

Italicized numbers refer to the annotated list.

Birding the
Delaware Valley
Region